# Equipping
# the Saints

# Equipping the Saints

## Best Practices in Contextual Theological Education

**David O. Jenkins** and
**P. Alice Rogers,** *editors*

THE
PILGRIM
PRESS
Cleveland

The Pilgrim Press
700 Prospect Avenue
Cleveland, Ohio 44115-1100
thepilgrimpress.com

14  13  12  11  10    5  4  3  2  1

Library of Congress Cataloging-in-Publication Data

Equipping the saints : best practices in contextual theological education /
David O. Jenkins and P. Alice Rogers, editors.
    p.  cm.
   Proceedings of a conference held in Sept. 2007 at Candler School of
Theology, Emory University.
   Includes bibliographical references.
   ISBN 978-0-8298-1860-4 (alk. paper)
   1. Pastoral theology – Fieldwork – Congresses.  I. Jenkins, David
Omar, 1953-  II. Rogers, P. Alice, 1961-
BV4164.5.E68 2010
230.071′ – dc22                                        2009037037

# Contents

Acknowledgments        ix

Foreword, *Walter Brueggemann*        xi

Introduction, *P. Alice Rogers*        1

### Part One
### INSTITUTIONAL VALUES
### THAT SHAPE BEST PRACTICES

1. The Evolution of Theological Field Education        11
   *Emily Click, Harvard Divinity School*

2. Individualism, Social Analysis, and Ministry Formation        24
   *Phil Campbell, Iliff School of Theology*

3. Bringing the City to Light: Pastoral Formation in a        40
   Multicultural Urban Context
   *Martha R. Jacobs, Eleanor Moody-Shepherd,*
   *Rebeca M. Radillo, New York Theological Seminary*

4. Intercultural Immersions within Contextual Education        49
   *Joseph S. Tortorici, Wesley Theological Seminary*

5. An Ethic of Risk at the School of the Prophets        60
   *Viki Matson, Vanderbilt Divinity School*

6. Teaching Congregations Initiative: A Paradigm for          68
   Forming Church Leaders in Mission-Shaped
   Communities
       *H. Stanley Wood, San Francisco Theological Seminary*

7. Contextualizing the Curriculum: The Communal and          85
   Integrative Practices of Theological Education
       *David O. Jenkins and P. Alice Rogers,*
       *Candler School of Theology*

## Part Two
## BEST PRACTICES
## OF SUPERVISION AND REFLECTION

8. Mentoring for Leadership                                   99
       *Lynn Rhodes, Pacific School of Religion*

9. Bridging Classroom and Parish: The Role of Supervision    107
       *Mark Diemer, Landis Coffman, Ruth Fortis,*
       *Jane Jenkins, Trinity Lutheran Seminary*

10. How Not to Praise Your Intern: The Role of Observation    117
    in Ministerial Formation
        *Barbara J. Blodgett, Yale Divinity School*

11. Constructive Congregational Feedback: Teaching            127
    Ministry Students and Congregations to Listen Well
    to One Another
        *Loletta Barrett, Karen Dalton, Karen Clark Ristine,*
        *Claremont School of Theology*

12. The Use of Selected Texts for Theological Reflection      139
    for Ministry
        *Mary Anne A. Bellinger, Michael I. N. Dash,*
        *Betty R. Jones, Interdenominational Theological Center*

13. Reflective Theological Leaders 150
   *W. J. Bryan III, Isabel N. Docampo, Barry E. Hughes,*
   *Thomas W. Spann, Perkins School of Theology*

Conclusion, *David O. Jenkins* 165

Bibliography 171

Contributors 175

# Acknowledgments

W E ARE GRATEFUL to the individuals and schools that so generously hosted us during our visits to discover the best practices of our peers. Their fundamental commitment to provide the best preparation possible for any person preparing for ministry was evident in their willingness to share their experience, their resources, and their wisdom.

We are also grateful to the individuals who contributed to this volume. In the midst of leading training sessions, interviewing students, and vetting ministry sites, they took the time to place on paper what they practice and experience on a daily basis.

We offer special thanks to Holly Butkovich and Jessica Smith, who worked tirelessly to bring together the seventeen seminaries for the national conference "Equipping the Saints: Best Practices in Contextual Theological Education." We also are indebted to Jessica Smith and Carmen Thompson for their administrative work on this volume.

Finally, we offer our deepest gratitude to Lilly Endowment, Inc., for its generous support and partnership. It makes possible the efforts in which we all engage to achieve for excellence in preparing future ministers for the work of the church in the world.

# Foreword

THIS IMPORTANT COLLECTION of reports and reflections offers a measure of the deep crisis faced in theological education, as well as the rich ferment that is underway in response to that crisis. Everyone can see that we face an immense crisis, as the old assumptions that have ordered power and knowledge among us no longer pertain. That deep social crisis with the fraying of our neighborly infrastructure is a wake-up call to the church in the United States, that there can be no more business as usual. And when there is such a loud wake-up call to the church, it gets the attention of theological educators, so that "no more business as usual" is a mantra in contemporary theological education.

The problem, of course, is that no one in the church or in seminary knows now how to undertake the new modes of business that pertain to and have creditability in a postmodern society that is without apparent order and is passionately committed to dumbing down. For that reason, these essays are to be appreciated, offered by practitioners who take the challenge seriously and are willing to experiment and run risks in new directions.

It is important to recognize that the general context for these reflections is "practical theology," that is, a reflection on the actual, concrete practice of ministry in and for and with the church. And while there are other possible venues for such practice, it is evident that the local congregation is the primary venue, because it is there that the raw edges of humanness (as every pastor knows) and the concreteness of missional energy are best situated.

These bold practitioners understand that the future of theological education must be *engagement* in a more immediate and direct sense with lived reality than the classical models of theological education have understood. As a consequence, whether one favors an emphasis on supervision or context or mentoring, it is all about face-to-face engagement with students-in-training that parallels and reiterates the face-to-face engagement that constitutes the fulcrum of ministry.

This book teems with rich suggestion for how such nurture in ministry might be better done. Four points in particular strike me about the new horizons probed here:

+ Practical theology of this sort is intensely *dialogical.* This of course is not new, but classical models of theological education have been dialogical only by accident. By dialogue one does not necessarily mean all sitting in a circle and "sharing." More than that, it refers to an engagement with the other whereby one is put at risk, impacted, and likely changed. Such a dialogic undertaking echoes Marx's aphorism, that we have talked long enough and now it is time to change the world. The change that first may happen is the changing of the parties to the dialogue.

+ Such engagement has to do with *the wholeness of the person* engaged with the wholeness of other persons, to some extent overcoming the old bifurcation of concept and emotion. In fact none of us ever reaches very far in such overcoming, but we keep working at the prospect.

+ I like the phrase *cultural competence* as a way to refer to the capacity to read and take seriously not only the individual person, but a thick network of cultural gifts and baggage, all of which each of us carries at all times. This awareness offers a huge challenge, because none of us ever attains such competence, either in self-discernment or in responding to the thick reality of the other. But it is the task in any case.

+ *Mission-shaped* is of course a major commitment, but when taken seriously it involves a profound unlearning. I suspect that the unlearning is acute for many who "sign up" for ministry, because models of church and ministry that still have compelling power have much more to do with equilibrium, maintenance, and custodial care than with missionally shaped life.

On all counts, this cadre of practical theologians in the art of practice constitute a scouting party of prophetic dimension. They probe out in front what might be embraced by all parties in the task of theological education. It is clear that this prophetic cadre will need many allies in the project of field-based learning.

Thus I suggest that the next two volumes to come after this volume of essays might concern the following:

First, practical theologians might pay close attention to the identification, recruitment, and solidarity with colleagues who occupy the more "classical disciplines" in the theological curriculum. I think it is unfortunate that this volume includes no blow-back from such colleagues. There are, of course, varieties of gifts, and other colleagues do not do what these colleagues do. But there are colleagues in other disciplines who know about and practice dialogic engagement, so that the learning may be an engagement with a transformative other. Until these colleagues are seen as allies, these practitioners will remain an isolated voice of advocacy. I think such alliance constitutes some hard work that now awaits practical theologians in field-based education.

Second, these essays stay largely at the level of process, and I understand why. But follow-up is now needed to ask, "To what end?" To what purpose is supervision, mentoring, or contextual accent? To answer this, the next collection of essays will have to focus on substantive issues of the nature of the church in this society, the shape and cost of mission, and the skills needed. There is a hint of this with reference to "social analysis," but the practitioners will have to risk articulation of an economic vision of how far to go with the radicality of the gospel and the dream of a transformed world. The colleagues who practice the arts of supervision and mentoring, in my view, will have to become more vigorous advocates for the content of faith and ministry that is to be carried by these processes.

I was particularly taken by the essay of Barbara Blodgett, who warns against "praising the intern" for the proper performance of ministerial tasks. The caution she offers in this regard seems to me the epitome of what must be faced in theological education and ministry. It is the recognition that effective performance in ministry is not cause for congratulations, but it is normal, routine, and expected. Her words call to mind Ed Friedman's judgment that ministers need too much to be liked and admired, rather than recognizing the reality of hard risk that belongs to faith. Thus behind Blodgett's discussion is a summons to redefine the culture of the church and its ministry that calls for the stamina and resolve for the regime change to which we witness. Servants are not rewarded by their masters simply for doing their duty. As every effective minister knows, after all the praise and applause, it is a sense of doing it well that permits the joy to match the cost of discipleship.

When one thinks about the changes that have to come about in theological education, one might almost despair about getting from here to there. That, moreover, reminds me of an occasion in the administration of the notorious governor of Georgia Lester Maddox. Maddox did a probe of prison reform in Georgia and concluded that the only way forward was "to get a better grade of prisoner." One might wish for a better grade of theological educator than the ones who will be allies in this pressing mandate. Or one might wish for a better grade of theological student. But, of course, neither of these is likely to happen. The hope is that these bold practitioners will continue this urgent advocacy, to summon allies to this vision, and to infiltrate and transform the whole enterprise. And then, when they do that, we will remember not to praise them too much.

Walter Brueggemann

*Columbia Theological Seminary*

# Introduction

## P. ALICE ROGERS

**W**HEN I FIRST ENTERED parish ministry as an ordained United Methodist elder, at least once a month the district superintendent called a meeting of all the ministers serving in my district. We gathered to fellowship, worship, and conduct the business of the district. I remember one of these district meetings in particular, because my district superintendent introduced me to a way of engaging with colleagues across my vocation that would strengthen and enhance my practice of ministry. He held up one of my denomination's magazines and said, "Each month, when I receive my *Interpreter's Magazine,* before I read any of the articles, I turn to the very back of the volume and read the submissions under the monthly column 'It Worked for Us.' " He went on to explain that these submissions were provided each month by pastors serving churches who were eager to share their creative ideas and strategies for ministry that worked in their particular contexts. He encouraged us to read that column each month, because in it we might find ideas that would invigorate and renew the ministry in our own churches. At that moment, as a young pastor I was introduced to the value of sharing "best practices" with others engaged in Christian ministry.

This sharing of best practices was new to me. Fresh from the academy, I was careful to abstain from any practice that might look like plagiarism. I had been taught that my work should be my own. My ideas should be original. Any thought, concept, or opinion that was not entirely my own should be footnoted. I should never share my work or borrow from others in such a way that it could be construed as cheating. It had been hammered into my head since first grade not to let anyone copy my answers, and by all means I should never copy from someone else. Now that I was engaged in full-time ministry, I was being encouraged by my district superintendent to *steal* others' best ideas. And not only that, these ministers were letting me "look on their paper" by sharing their "answers" in a denominational publication!

For the next twenty years, I followed the advice of that district superintendent. When I received my *Interpreter's Magazine,* I turned first to "It Worked for Us," and I read the ideas and suggestions submitted by those hard at work serving the local church. I also learned the importance and value of gathering with other ministers in my district, as well as those from other denominations in my community, to discuss sermon preparation, ways to engage the community, approaches to congregational leadership, etc. I learned that the habit of sharing best practices served to strengthen the ministry of the church in the world.

When I reentered the academy as a theological field educator, I discovered that many professional schools of theology engaged in this very custom of sharing best practices. The same rigorous academic standards were required for serious study and research; however, because we were responsible for the formation and training of educated practitioners, like the schools of nursing, law, and medicine, it was clear that sharing best practices among our peers was essential to our common mission.

Candler School of Theology had already begun the process of curricular revision when I arrived in 2002, and as codirectors of the Contextual Education program, David Jenkins and I were charged with the task of evaluating our model for this program. To that end, David and I wrote to many of our peer institutions and requested the opportunity to visit with them to observe their Contextual or Field Education programs and to speak with those involved. Over the next three years, we visited thirteen seminaries with the express purpose of observing their best practices. In each visit, we were overwhelmed by the generous hospitality of our peers. They readily made available their manuals, evaluation tools, and training materials. They scheduled conversations with site supervisors, students, faculty, and academic deans. They arranged visits to their ecclesial, social, and clinical sites. Each school shared with us the ways in which it prepares and forms students for the practice of ministry in the world.

We discovered that while all schools maintained the common goal of preparing students for ministerial service, they were engaged in unique and creative practices they had developed in response to this goal in their particular contexts and institutions. The institutional values inherent in the seminaries or the school's denomination shaped many programs, commitment to particular practices shaped others, and the contexts in which schools are located informed their models. David and I were fascinated with these nuances of the shared goals of Contextual Theological Education, and we were convinced that the directors of these programs should have the opportunity to share their values, ideas, and practices with one another in such a way that these practices could be disseminated to a larger audience.

In September 2007, through a generous grant from the Lilly Endowment, Inc., Candler School of Theology hosted a national conference entitled, "Equipping the Saints: Best Practices in Contextual Theological Education." Representatives of seventeen seminaries from across the country gathered to present papers on one practice evidenced in their contextual or field education programs. Each seminary had the opportunity to bring a team of up to four persons, so many schools brought students, site mentors, and teaching supervisors. The consultation provided space for enthusiastic conferencing and creative collaboration as each school shared distinct aspects of its program. The papers from that conference are collected in this volume as a record of those presentations and as a means to disseminate the values and practices that shape contextual theological education.

## *Overview of the Book*

The authors of these chapters are engaged in contextual theological field education. On a daily basis they are focused on the practices of ministry, the formation of students for ministry, and the supervision of those engaged in the various programs. They are engaged in the theoretical work of theological education and also the hands-on practice and formation for ministry. They write from their particular contexts, while offering practices that can easily inform models of contextual education in other contexts.

In part 1, Emily Click sets the stage for the chapters that follow as she outlines three models through which most seminaries teach students to become reflective practitioners: the Mentoring Model, the Theologically Reflecting Model, and the Integrating Model. She provides a framework by which the reader may locate the values and practices offered by each seminary. For instance, several chapters focus on issues of mentoring, but those practices are approached differently based on the model in which they are located. An understanding of these models allows one to envision creative ways in which these practices may be adapted.

Many of the papers presented at the conference revealed institutional values that shape their contextual and field education programs. Those values may be driven by denominational beliefs and requirements for ordination, they may arise from the context in which the school exists, or they may emerge from historical events that transformed the seminary. Whatever their origin, they are values that shape the way some seminaries approach contextual education.

The contexts in which our seminaries reside could easily allow students to perpetuate the assumptions of individualism. Conscious of this contextual challenge, the field education program at Iliff advances the role of social analysis as a means to help students understand the ways in which they are shaped by their communities and social contexts. Phil Campbell argues that explicit attention to social analysis is crucial for a student's formation for ministry, especially for students who are members of the dominant culture.

The multicultural context in which New York Theological Seminary resides presents a unique opportunity for preparing students for ministry. The student body, as well as the city in which it is located, is extremely diverse, and New York Theological Seminary has shaped its Supervised Ministry program to address the preparation of students in a context where diversity is valued. As we see in the chapter presented by Martha R. Jacobs, Eleanor Moody-Shepherd, and Rebeca M. Radillo, the operating value that underlies all of their practices is "all are welcome at the table."

Joseph Tortorici describes the practice at Wesley Theological Seminary, which provides students with the opportunity to be immersed in a culture quite different from their own. His essay focuses on the values held by Wesley that shape the preparation of students for a ministry that will inevitably bring them face to face with persons and groups of other cultures.

Historical experience, an architectural artifact, and modern-day commitments provide the guiding values for the field education program at Vanderbilt Divinity School. Viki Matson recounts the controversy that surrounded the admission of James Lawson in the 1960s, describes an artifact identifying Vanderbilt Divinity School as a "School of the Prophets," and enumerates the current commitments held by the school to implement the institutional value of risk-taking that shapes its field education program. Inherent in their practice is the conviction that if the world is to be transformed, then those engaged in the transformation must be prepared to take risks for that transformation to be realized.

The placement of students in congregations equipped to transform the world as mission-shaped communities is the focus of H. Stanley Wood's chapter. He provides the theological understanding of mission-shaped communities that forms the criteria by which San Francisco Theological Seminary recruits congregations to serve as site placements for students. He then offers a specific example of a mission-shaped congregation that participates in SFTS's Teaching Congregation Initiative. We overhear the commitments of the site supervisor and the experience of the student as they reflect on their participation in this model.

As Candler School of Theology engaged in its curriculum revision, the commitment to the contextualization of the curriculum was central. The restructuring of the Contextual Education program modeled this commitment. In chapter 7, David Jenkins and I discuss the ways in which the formation that students experience in social, clinical, and ecclesial settings are integrated across the disciplines. The faculty's commitment to this institutional value shaped this model in which students' engagement in the Contextual Education program is not marginalized, but rather integrated across the entire curriculum.

Part 2 highlights particular practices presented by the seminaries at the conference that have strengthened their programs in contextual and field education. For instance, no program denies the fundamental value of the role of supervision in contextual field education placements. However, schools approach their engagement with these practitioners in different ways. With thirty-five years of experience and leadership in this discipline, Lynn Rhodes describes the intentional focus placed on the selection and preparation of mentors at Pacific School of Theology. She speaks about the relationship the seminary has with the mentor, the relationship between the mentor and the student, and the relationship of the mentor with his or her own vocation. Rhodes also considers how the role of mentoring must anticipate changes in the church.

The work of site supervisors, students, faculty, congregations, and staff requires a high degree of collaboration. The authors of the chapter written by Trinity Lutheran Seminary exemplify such collegiality. Together they focus on the ways in which the site supervisor provides a bridge between the traditional seminary disciplines and the daily realities of parish ministry. Jane Jenkins and Ruth Fortis offer a thick description of their program. Two pastors, Mark Diemer and Landis Coffman, follow with a description of how that program and its training is experienced and practiced.

Many seminaries struggle to train site supervisors in effective student assessment. Judicatories often require seminaries to provide evaluations of a student's practical work, contextual and field education programs need to assess student performance, and it is imperative that students receive feedback on their site work. However, in a profession that values encouragement and affirmation, it is often hard to move site supervisors beyond giving praise to the more difficult exercise of critique through observation. Barbara Blodgett's work focuses on this practice. Her research suggests that praise of seemingly fixed qualities such as intelligence or compassion reinforces in learners a mindset that actually stunts their growth and formation. She offers the Observation Report as a tool for strengthening the evaluative role of site supervisors.

The relationship between the site supervisor and the student is not the only relationship experienced in ecclesial field education placements. The student's relationship with the congregation also is critical and plays a significant role in the mentoring and formation of a student. Claremont School of Theology highlights its practice of developing and training lay committees for this critical work. In chapter 11 Loletta Barrett, Karen Dalton, and Karen Clark Ristine explore the relevance of lay committees, offer narratives from participants, and provide practical ways for organizing and training lay committees.

A different set of relationships drives the practice of using selected texts for theological reflection at Interdenominational Theological Seminary. Mary Anne A. Bellinger, Michael I. N. Dash, and Betty R. Jones offer this practice as a means for training students to be self-evaluative, critical theologians. The pedagogical model they describe challenges students to examine how their personal experiences are shaped through the interrelated relationships between pre-text, texts, and contexts for ministry.

A practice that students at Perkins School of Theology learn for this work is the writing of theological reflection papers with special attention to "mega theological discourse." In chapter 13 W. J. Bryan III, Isabel N. Docampo, Barry E. Hughes, and Thomas W.

Spann describe the challenges and strengths of this practice and offer important questions that all engaged in preparing students for ministry should consider.

While these few chapters offer only a brief glimpse into the world of contextual theological field education, one can readily see the willingness of those engaged in this important work to share what they have discovered, to build upon what has proved successful, and to continue seeking ways to prepare students for ministry in an ever changing world. While none of us would suggest that plagiarism is acceptable or that taking credit for another's ideas is ethical, we offer this volume as a means to continue the conversations about the best practices that "worked for us," and to share ways in which future leaders can be shaped and formed for ministry.

# PART ONE

# Institutional Values That Shape Best Practices

# - 1 -

# The Evolution of Theological Field Education

## EMILY CLICK

### Harvard Divinity School

O VER THE PAST SIXTY YEARS, theological field education (TFE) has become a critically important part of the master of divinity curriculum. Field education's role has shifted away from primarily administrative work that involved tracking the details of placing divinity students in church-related work. Such work generally was considered distinct from academic study. Over the years, field education programs have gradually moved into a role of implementing multiple educational components crucial to integrating the overall master of divinity curriculum.[1] This chapter provides a framework for understanding the newly complex landscape of field education. It is hoped that this framework will then enable readers to interpret subsequent chapters as they describe particular practices within field education and will explore ways such practices fit into the overall purposes of field education.

---

1. The Association for Theological Field Education (ATFE) began its biennial meetings sixty years ago. At that time a small group of field educators began meeting to develop greater awareness about the educational potential in what was then largely viewed as work on the side, unrelated to learning in the classroom environment. They worked together to shift perceptions and actual experiences toward claiming those experiences as learning opportunities. That was when the phrase "field education" supplanted "field work." However, the perception that students are applying theory through taking church jobs, or making money by doing work for the church part time, rather than engaging in the very learning that will serve to integrate the rest of their theoretical studies, persists even today.

This evolution within field education relates to broader shifts within education in general. During this same period, new educational theories emerged that emphasized the value of integrating practice in contexts with classroom learning. Foremost among these educational theorists was Paulo Freire, who pointed to the role of praxis in education. His development of these epistemological understandings has strengthened the ability of field educators to make the case for the crucial importance of engaging students in work that generates mutually informative interactions between theoretical and contextualized learning experiences.[2] Yet during this time when field education has developed from a marginalized supplementary work program into a crucial integrative aspect of a degree, strikingly little has been written about the actual practices of TFE.[3] The time has come for field educators to examine their crucial role in the integrative work within theological education.

The 2007 conference sponsored by Candler School of Theology provided valuable concrete data about how field educators currently are doing this work of creating integrative learning opportunities in their diverse theological school settings. The Candler conference, "Equipping the Saints," highlighted best practices within theological field education. This gathering of field educators explored how different programs engage students in international field settings, social justice sites, and a range of other programmatic emphases that foster excellent student learning.

---

2. Paulo Freire's book *Pedagogy of the Oppressed* (New York: Continuum, 1981), established the impossibility of teaching students in a way that is actually divorced from context; all learning is contextual. Freire ignited a lively conversation that continues today about how practice in context is shaped by and also informs "theoretical" work. He uses the word "praxis" to denote an inseparable connection between action and reflection. Since Freire's publication of this highly influential text educators in many fields have worked to engage students in activities that connect with the theoretical aspects of their course work. These general developments in educational theory have made it easier to recognize the ways in which field education works as one crucial component for contextualizing learning within the M.Div. curriculum.

3. My own dissertation, "Forming Religious Leaders through Theological Field Education," summarizes contemporary practices within TFE. The dissertation is available through dissertation abstracts.

The Candler conference provided a stunning sampling of the creative diversity within TFE in its sixth decade of existence. The conference, however, did not establish a paradigm for how field education should be done in every institutional setting. The diversity and creativity embodied in the conference presentations reflects an emerging reality within TFE: we are pursuing varied educational goals under the common title "field education." Because of this range of purposes, it is a complex task to determine which approaches and practices represent excellence in preparing ministers.

Field educators, for example, often encounter judicatories examining the issue of how much of a student's field educational work should take place within a congregational context. These denominational officials may, in some cases, be weighing the obvious advantages and disadvantages of work in social justice ministries, or in international settings, against the direct evidence of demonstrable learning when students prepare for service in the particular context of the parish. There are no clear guidelines of what should be included in nonparish settings that would make these field education sites equally valuable as learning contexts for those aiming at congregational leadership. This type of issue points to the value of the Candler conference, which offered specific examples of best practices and demonstrated ways particular programs have built in expectations and guidelines to meet the learning goals of their students and the needs of their constituents.

In highlighting such a diversity of practices, the Candler conference suggests that we have yet to answer definitively the question of which are and which are not the best practices in particular institutional settings. What we know is that we are doing varied things in different programs, and we interpret the goals of field education differently depending on our contexts, our missional purposes, and our student populations. Yet it is still possible to provide an interpretive framework for understanding and evaluating these varied practices within TFE, and it is still advantageous to imagine which practices might represent excellence in equipping saints.

This chapter outlines a way for us to interpret differences between programs so that we might find ways to engage the important questions of how best to prepare students for ministerial service. Therefore, this chapter differs from the others in a significant way. Instead of focusing on a singular practice that represents one form of excellence within theological field education, this chapter supplies an overview of the entire landscape of TFE. It sets up this comparative paradigm by summarizing the findings of my Ph.D. dissertation, which explored how various TFE programs are structured. That study took place over a six-year period and was presented to the annual gathering of field educators in Toronto in 2005.[4]

The central finding of this study was that TFE programs can be loosely clustered into three main models based on the degree to which they emphasize one of three elements found in nearly every TFE program. These three models provide the interpretive framework for the emerging diversity of practices within TFE, so vibrantly represented by the presentations at Candler. It is my conviction that this developing diversity is a strength signifying the maturing educational culture of TFE.

Before I describe the three major models of field education, it is helpful to summarize the major purpose of field education. In my study I state that the major purpose is to teach ministerial reflection. This term is intentionally broader than the more frequently used term "theological reflection." Most field educators state that their programs engage students in theological reflection; however, what is meant by theological reflection varies greatly between institutions. In one program, theological reflection might focus on what a student understands about him- or herself as a leader in a faith community, while in another program the emphasis might focus on building a student's skills in identifying what a community articulates as its missional purpose. Thus my own study moved away from summarizing the purpose of TFE as "theological reflection" and instead pointed to a broader type of reflection and called it

---

4. The address is available on the Association for Theological Field Education website: *www.atfe.org*.

"ministerial reflection." This term includes theological reflection, skill building, and the growth of self-understanding, each a part of the umbrella purpose of fostering ministerial reflection within TFE.[5]

Field education programs teach ministerial reflection in three different ways. These models are based on the degree of focus placed upon the three major educational elements found in nearly every program. These educational elements are the supervisor, the peer reflective seminar or practicum, and the integration of field-based learning with other aspects of the curriculum. TFE programs tend to give the most weight to one of these elements, yet nearly all programs draw on all three aspects with varying weight given to one or the other. There are three broad models for how programs give weight to these elements as they structure their TFE programs: the Reflection through Supervision Model, the Reflection through Seminar (or Practicum) Model, and the Reflection through Curricular Integration Model. One can identify TFE programs by their preference for one of these models. The study concluded that no one model necessarily is inherently superior to the others, except that in any given school one model might be a better match for the missional purpose of the larger institution.

The first major educational context is the supervisory relationship. Usually this is a relationship between clergy and the student, but lay persons may be the primary supervisors; or in the case of social justice work or in some faith traditions, the supervisor may or may not be ordained clergy. This supervisory relationship is crucial in every field education program, but in some it is regarded as the core, the primary and ultimate learning environment.

In other programs the primary emphasis is placed on the way the learning in context is set into an interpretive framework via

---

5. Donald A. Schön's book *Educating the Reflective Practitioner: Toward a New Design for Teaching and Learning in the Professions* (San Francisco: Jossey-Bass, 1987) has informed an entire generation of field educators on the importance in any profession of inculcating reflection as a part of excellent professional practice. Schön clarifies that excellent professionals reflect while in action in tacit ways, and also develop more intentional strategies for reflecting after action in ways that inform them with regard to improving their professional practices.

a reflective seminar, often led by a member of the teaching faculty or by specially trained adjunct faculty. These seminars usually take place on campus and meet in an environment of cultivated trust and facilitated sharing. The purposes of these seminars vary from developing student self-awareness, to engendering theological reflection, to building emotional intelligences. These seminars develop the ability of students to engage in learning with their peers.

The final element is the integration of the field education with the rest of the M.Div. curriculum. The integration of the work and learning in field education makes it inseparable from the learning embedded throughout the curriculum. Field education permeates the educational culture and supplies experiences and reflective tools that vitalize the overall curriculum.

Every program references the value of all three of these elements. Each program values supervisors, for example. One would not want to engage students in a context without excellent supervision, nor to devalue the importance of the expertise of the practitioners and the need for them to actually instruct students on what ministry is all about. Yet for some programs this relationship between supervisors and students is nearly the totality of what field education is intended to be, while for others it constitutes one crucial part of field education. Similarly, all schools encourage reflection with peers on field education experiences. Every school hopes that its curriculum is integrated to some degree and recognizes that field education plays a vital role in achieving such integration. Schools differ primarily in the degree of emphasis placed on each element.

In the Reflecting through Supervision Model, the strongest value is placed on learning in context. The key question for field educators is how to support and select excellent supervisors and how to enable students to receive full advantage from immersion into a setting they consider superior for learning. Thus, these educators sometimes emphasize the value of full-time internships that take place away from the seminary. These programs often defer to the expertise of the congregation, because they recognize that seminaries cannot and indeed should not replicate the particular type of knowing, mentoring, and functioning of congregations.

In contrast to the Supervisory Model, the Reflection through Seminar Model emphasizes the importance of interpreting and reflecting upon contextualized experiences. In these programs, students still engage in context and reflect with their supervisors. Yet students also learn to write case studies or verbatims for further reflection in a seminar setting, usually expertly facilitated by someone skilled at enabling learning that reframes assumptions and underlying understandings. Often this structure even includes reflection upon the supervisory relationship in a way that builds students' self-understandings about their reactions to authority and power. These programs usually tolerate a diversity of theological perspectives and simply encourage students to develop their own coherent theological perspectives while allowing perspectives different from their own.

In programs that operate in the Reflection through Seminar Model, the key question for field educators is how best to constitute the seminars, support the seminar leaders, and develop a curriculum for the seminars that supports learning for ministerial formation. These programs seek exemplary texts for teaching theological reflection and training and evaluating seminar leaders. Some programs assert that regular faculty should teach or facilitate these seminars, so that they are not seen as marginal work carried out by less qualified faculty. Others view this as work for which full-time teaching faculty might or might not be qualified, and instead place value on cultivating teachers who specialize in facilitating ministerial reflection in a group context.

This decision about who best teaches seminars is one area where a diversity of practices might represent excellence depending on the key mission and purpose of the institution. In some institutions, including full-time faculty in teaching seminars might be best. In other settings, excellence might be achieved through engaging practitioners in adjunct teaching that focuses on developing the particular art of ministerial reflection.

These first two models — the Reflection through Supervision Model and the Reflection through Seminar Model — comprise the vast majority of programs in existence today. But an intriguing third approach is emerging in a number of settings and represents an approach that is sufficiently different as to warrant a third model: the Reflection through Curricular Integration Model. In these programs, the work that students do in context, and even in peer seminars, is valued in the way that field education supplies crucial learning throughout the curriculum. In these institutions, an Old Testament professor, for example, might find it difficult to instruct students on the core content of her course without referencing the way that content comes alive in the context of ministerial engagement. She might assign students to teach the creation stories of Genesis in their field education settings and report back on the questions and insights that emerged from the teaching process. In these institutions, the accomplishment of any aspect of the M.Div. curriculum depends, in a crucial way, upon the student being engaged in a ministry setting which demands ministerial action as well as reflection.

In programs that operate with the Reflection through Curricular Integration Model, the key question for field educators is how to deepen integrative learning opportunities throughout the curriculum. This may, for example, call faculty to imagine how to contextualize learning throughout the coursework. Or it may call for adding discussion sessions to existing coursework. While the field educator in this setting may administer a program that outwardly appears similar to those in the other models, he or she may preclude a seminar structure believing that such structures reinforce the marginalization of learning through field education.

Over the past few years, I have presented these models to field educators and deans from various institutions. Most have immediately recognized how they would characterize their own school. On more than one occasion, these respondents seemed to wistfully prefer the third model as obviously superior. However, while all three models have valuable aspects, each might also have characteristics that would make it less than ideal for a given institution. I caution respondents against jumping to an immediate conclusion about the suitability of a given model to their setting without first considering the relative strengths and drawbacks.

A brief summary of the strengths and drawbacks of each model will further clarify how they represent options for best practices, but there is still no paradigm. All three models have significant advantages as well as disadvantages. Ultimately, any institution must decide which weaknesses it will tolerate in order to garner the strengths of a given model.

In the Reflection through Supervision Model, students experience the advantage of engaging in the practice of ministry with timely instruction. For instance, the student preaches a provocative sermon, and she receives clear and immediate feedback from her supervisor. The superiority of this model lies in the way it steers clear of abstractions and idealistic thinking while engaging students in relationships and context. It is one thing to learn the main symptoms of depression; it is quite another to find the words or presence to comfort the person mired in grief over tragic loss. The major strength of this model is the way it emphasizes the value of learning in context and not in a setting removed from immediate engagement.

The Reflection through Supervision model emphasizes the ways that excellent learning occurs when novices have a mentor who can shape their developing ministry in response to actual challenges. This model recognizes that excellent instruction can occur when a learning partnership develops in which each partner is present to the same circumstances. The best supervisors do not seek to create clones; rather they shape students by modeling their own excellence in practice and encouraging students to develop their own abilities. There is a beauty in the ways that expert practitioners both instruct and learn from their junior learning partners and encourage the growth of new leaders through nuanced and highly focused tutoring in the situation.

One of the drawbacks to this Reflection through Supervision Model is that it is overly tied to context. There is little that can be done to correct a supervisor who, for example, undercuts the central instructions of the curriculum. Who has not heard a supervisor make a dismissive statement such as, "Oh you have to forget most of what you learn in seminary anyway"? Even more disconcerting are the supervisors who abuse their power to minimize the strengths of students in order to build up their own sense of superiority. While these cases are rare, this model can sometimes result in students navigating very difficult situations.

The Reflection through Supervision Model cultivates reflection in action and, to some extent, reflection after action. This model encourages reflection on the big picture, a skill that is very necessary; however, it is does not always provide opportunities for thorough social analytic reflection that is critical of assumptions, systems, and frameworks.[6] While it is possible for an excellent supervisor to engage students in these types of reflective moments, it is less likely to occur than in the other two models. This model has a bias toward reflection that is closely tied to action, which has its corresponding strengths and weaknesses.

The strengths of the second model, Reflection through Seminar, lie in its distance from action. Presumably students still engage in reflection in action, but this model ensures that they also will engage in the more intentional and thorough reflection that comes through regularly scheduled sessions that require preparation, forethought, and intense engagement with input from others with varying perspectives. One could, for example, imagine that a student and

---

6. In his highly influential text, *Leadership without Easy Answers* (Cambridge, Mass.: Belknap Press of Harvard University Press, 1994), Ronald Heifetz writes of the importance of navigating what he calls adaptive challenges. These are the types of problems that are not clearly defined, and do not have readily identifiable, technical answers. Heifetz asserts that today's leaders must develop skills to engage people, or mobilize them, for adaptive challenges. While his book is not written specifically with religious leaders in mind, many field educators and theological educators have recognized that the ways in which he describes leadership illuminate precisely the types of swamp-like problems religious institutions face today.

supervisor would develop a Christian Education program using an approach that they both fail to recognize as discriminatory against persons with disabilities. It could be that only when the student presents the program in the context of a group of peers that he or she receives feedback indicating that the program is problematic. Similarly, a student may become locked in a power battle with a supervisor, from which they can receive release only when a peer points out their roles in setting up the problematic dynamics. Thus, this model has strengths that may bring needed balance and perspective to students once they reflect in groups removed from context.

This second model's strength has its attendant weaknesses as well. One can imagine a situation in which a group of students becomes convinced that the correct stance is to be prophetic and encourages a fellow student to charge into the context with an agenda of proclaiming The Truth. Yet no one in that group actually knows the situation as well as the supervisor and lay persons, and the whole group may be too tied to an ideal value without the corrective of knowing the actual circumstances. For example, students may be too busy to read the local newspaper. They may not realize that a community is highly sensitive to an escalating rate of teenage pregnancy, or drug use, or racial conflicts. They may develop a mentality that is inadequately informed by context, and thus the group does not necessarily function in a way that brings appropriate perspective. There is a real possibility that a group can reinforce problematic behavior and assumptions rather than challenging them. There is no guarantee that this model ensures adequate reflection, yet its strength lies in the way it usually combines at least two types of reflection and balances the dominance of immediacy with the challenge of reflection from diverse perspectives.

The third model also has its strengths and weaknesses. Its strength lies in its capacity to tie together otherwise disparate strands of learning. Edward Farley long ago said that the "clerical paradigm" is a result of a curriculum that fails at the crucial work of integration.[7] This third model can address this problem. The as yet unanswered question is whether this model fixes the problem or exacerbates it. The concern with the Integrative Model is locating where the learning occurs and assessing that learning. One can, for example, easily observe how students reflect on experience in the second model. In the first model one can read a written evaluation of the supervisory sessions. In this third model, it is difficult to name precisely where the integrative learning occurs. And this suggests it may be happening everywhere, or nowhere. If faculty, for example, claim they have contextualized their coursework, who is to say that such contextualization is sufficient for the preparation of ministers? In the example earlier cited, in which the Old Testament professor has students teach the creation story and bring reflections on their teaching, who is to say that the way the professor responds will actually prepare the students to engage in ministerial leadership? There also exists the potential that students will fail to report accurately, which then makes it highly problematic to receive helpful instruction.

This third model calls for an institution-wide commitment to learning how to instruct and how to establish praxis that engages theory and practice. One can imagine theological schools with faculty that could rise to this challenge, but given the demands of the guilds, it is difficult to imagine that every faculty person engaged in theological education is likely to view the integrative learning opportunity as necessarily his or her own calling. Thus, the preference for this third model, with its apparent accomplishment of the goal of curricular integration, should be tempered by a check against core institutional values and purposes.

---

7. In *Theologia: The Fragmentation and Unity of Theological Education* (Philadelphia: Fortress Press, 1983), Edward Farley describes the rather intractable problem of disunity within theological education. There has been much debate in the intervening years since the publication of this volume about whether field education exacerbates this problem or helps alleviate it. He refers to the discontent with theological education on the part of churches as misunderstanding the value of educating ministers theologically. There is little evidence that the past twenty-five years have brought resolution to Farley's "clerical paradigm."

These three models — Reflection through Supervision, Reflection through Seminar, and Reflection through Curricular Integration — represent diverse strategies from which institutions may choose for preparing religious leaders. Each model recognizes the importance of supplementing student experience with structured reflection. In the end, what matters most is not which model is selected, but the match between institutional values, the missional purpose of the educational program, and the field education program's approach. Each approach can encourage excellent practices for ministerial preparation, and, unfortunately, no approach protects absolutely against the potential for inadequate preparation. It remains for future conferences and writers to suggest ways to build strategies to teach tomorrow's leaders how to engage in ministry in emerging contexts.

# – 2 –

# Individualism, Social Analysis, and Ministry Formation

PHIL CAMPBELL

Iliff School of Theology

I N DOMINANT CULTURE PARLANCE, to be "American" is to define oneself as an individual and embrace and celebrate one's individual freedom. Likewise, to be "religious" is to have individual beliefs and to have a personal relationship with God. This individualist perspective is the starting point for many students, especially white middle-class students (the large majority of the student body) who enter the Iliff School of Theology.[1] These individualist assumptions consciously and unconsciously shape much of the Iliff discourse, including that regarding professional formation for ministry. Theological field education has the capacity to address this individualist ethos of the dominant culture as we prepare seminarians for leadership in the church.

This challenge is not unique to Iliff, nor is it an issue solely for the academy. Recently, I was the guest preacher for a Sunday morning worship service at a theologically moderate/liberal congregation in the Metro Denver area. During the service, a lay reader read the portion of Isaiah 58 that identifies an "acceptable fast" as the loosening of the bonds of injustice, freeing the oppressed, feeding the hungry and housing the homeless. The reader introduced the passage by

---

1. Over 80 percent of the Iliff student body is white.

explaining that Isaiah offered his community a social as well as religious agenda. Her comments indicated that she supported Isaiah's social agenda, but her contrasting "social" with "religious" pointed to the deeply entrenched individualism that shapes dominant culture perspectives in church and society.

Individualism, however, does not capture the totality of what it means to be religious or human. Persons are shaped by their communities and social contexts. Social analysis helps students decipher the systemic and structural dimensions of the issues and situations they face and can equip them for fuller and more effective engagement in social justice ministries. Given the individualism into which many students are consciously and unconsciously socialized, it will be argued that explicit attention to social analysis is crucial in order to deepen ministry formation that includes broader understandings of personhood and that fosters social awareness and action.

The individualism of the dominant narrative of the United States has been widely attested since Alexis de Tocqueville and is rooted in Lockean understandings of the autonomous self. In *Habits of the Heart: Individualism and Commitment in American Life,* Robert Bellah and his colleagues interviewed over two hundred persons in the United States who "in spite of their differences...share a common moral vocabulary, which we propose to call the 'first language' of American individualism."[2] The value of individualism is significant. The goal of helping persons become fully functioning individuals is an essential component of effective and compassionate pastoral care. Further, individualism has supported individual human rights and the value of dissent. Individualism can encourage nonconformist values consistent with the Gospel.[3] It has fostered

---

2. Robert Bellah et al., *Habits of the Heart: Individualism and Commitment in American Life* (Berkeley: University of California Press, 1985), 20. Significantly, all those interviewed are white, although virtually no mention of this is made in the study. The white experience is, unconsciously at least, equated with the American experience, and white individualism is implicitly posited as the American norm.

3. Romans 12:2: "Do not be conformed to this world but be transformed by the renewing of your minds."

a spirit of free inquiry and extended the freedoms to those whose individual worth is affirmed. Seeing persons as individuals rather than categorizing them by group can lead to greater involvement in church and society for those previously excluded because of gender, race, sexual orientation, physical ability, or some other essentializing condition.

Despite the gifts of individualism, however, it also has its limits. An individualist perspective can obscure very real social differences and discourage critical assessments of how systemic, structural, and institutional dynamics privilege some and oppress others. It can narrow the notion of what it means to be human and fail to take into account the ways that social history and communal context shape personhood and influence access to full participation in church and society, despite stated individual commitments to the contrary. Concerns about the limitations of individualism were identified by the *Habits of the Heart* researchers, who argue that individuals have become increasingly autonomous and isolated with regard to moral decision making. "In the course of our history the self has become more detached from the social and cultural contexts.... The current focus of a socially unsituated self from which all judgments are supposed to flow"[4] is the starting point for dominant culture reflection on human vocation. As this finding relates specifically to the Iliff context, socially unsituated individualism has been a prominent, if largely unconscious, paradigm for understanding professional formation. The importance of context and social location are unacknowledged or at least understated in most of the formal formation discourse at Iliff. Although significant reference is made to context and social location throughout the Iliff curriculum and the curriculum of many schools, imbedded individualistic assumptions remain ensconced and influence academic preparation and professional formation.

---

4. Bellah, *Habits of the Heart,* 55. Bellah et al. extend this critique in Robert Neely Bellah, *The Good Society* (New York: Vintage Books, 1992).

## *Individualism and Ministry Formation*

Individualist assumptions are reflected in the professional formation goals in the Iliff School of Theology's *Master's Student Handbook*. Professional formation includes:

- authentic presentation of self and experience;
- ability to maintain appropriate boundaries and to balance them with appropriate accessibility;
- a sense of commitment to one's spiritual development;
- a capacity to understand and employ the heritage and values of one's tradition;
- ability to be aware of one's inner subjective state and to meet the requirements of role and position;
- a sense of fair-mindedness and justice;
- an ability to clearly interpret one's beliefs and behavior to the community one serves;
- possession and development of skills for ministry (preaching, leadership, counseling, administration, etc.).

These goals address one's personal, spiritual and intrapsychic development and the ability to interpret individual beliefs to others. Whereas formation includes the "capacity to understand and employ the heritage and values of one's tradition," there is no explicit mention of the capacity to interpret contexts, appreciate the role of the community in understanding what it means to be human, or understand and integrate the importance of social location for either self-understanding or professional practice.[5] This description of formation suggests that what is essential, in addition to attaining the requisite skills and knowledge, is to deal with one's own concerns and issues so that these matters do not get in the way of relating to others. Whereas addressing one's personal concerns is crucial, there is little in these goals to suggest that these personal matters

---

5. The *Master's Student Handbook* for the 2007–8 academic year was updated to reflect the importance of understanding and appreciating context and social location.

are socially located or conditioned. Instead, it seems to imply that these issues are a part of the universal human condition.

Similar goals are evident in other prominent approaches to professional ministry formation, including Clinical Pastoral Education (CPE) and family systems theory. Many denominational judicatories expect ministry candidates to engage in CPE as well as field education, although the value of CPE is often presented as culturally neutral. Practitioners of color, however, have challenged this assertion, critiquing CPE's unexamined individualism and white cultural particularity. "Individualism is the central organizing cultural assumption that underlies clinical pastoral education.... Unreflective whiteness intensifies individualism in the supervisory process, making it very difficult for the supervisor to understand the experience and behavior of the student who is culturally different from the supervisor."[6] Further, CPE assumes that self-understanding is deepened by reflecting on one's individual history and experience rather than exploring the community in which one is embedded.[7]

Individualism is also prominent in family systems theory as manifest in the Bowens school and popularized for congregational application in Friedman's *Generation to Generation*. With regard to ministry formation, there is much to be gained from exposure to Bowens's approach regarding the dangers of overfunctioning, unhealthy enmeshment, shared anxiety, etc. But its assumptions are rooted in individualist understandings that emphasize differentiation, which is one's "capacity... to define his or her own life goals and values apart from surrounding togetherness pressures, to say 'I' when others are demanding 'you' and 'we.' "[8] It is further assumed that all systems work in similar ways. How systems are embedded in larger systems and how social dynamics of race and class

---

6. Therese M. Becker, "Individualism and the Invisibility of Monoculturalism/Whiteness: Limits to Effective Clinical Pastoral Education Supervision," *Journal of Supervision and Training in Ministry* (October 2002): 5.

7. Ibid., 7ff. CPE assumptions are not static or monolithic. Becker's critique notwithstanding, the role of context and culture is under examination in the CPE discourse. Contextual and intercultural awareness is growing.

8. Edwin H. Friedman, *Generation to Generation: Family Process in Church and Synagogue* (New York: Guilford Press, 1985), 27.

impact the family system are not addressed. It is beyond the scope of this chapter to engage in either critique or defense of the value of Bowen's and Friedman's insights. Instead, I suggest here that they are socially located and that their particularity, as opposed to universality, is often unacknowledged in dominant culture discourse regarding ministry formation. Further, the individualist assumption of family systems theory can be particularly problematic for those with a more communal understanding of personhood. The racial dimension of this difference can be overstated, but whites generally have a more individual orientation and people of color a more communal one. It is the difference between the Cartesian, "I think therefore I am," and the African, "I am because we are."

Individualism presents a challenge for professional formation in other fields as well as ministry. Sharon Parks has reflected on the challenges of teaching ethics at the Harvard School of Business with students who have been socialized into dominant culture assumptions that relegate ethical reflection to the realm of the interpersonal.[9] Parks found that most incoming graduate business students were predisposed to seeing only familial or interpersonal concerns as relevant for ethical reflection. They assumed that modes of production, what products to manufacture or sell, how business practices affect the environment and the economy, workplace conditions, etc., were all driven by market conditions rather than ethical commitments. The business school's ethics curriculum was designed to enlarge ethical reflection by introducing systemic analysis. "An interpersonal ethic of trustworthiness and mutual accountability is essential but not sufficient for ethical managerial practice."[10] Parks discovered that her students "have a vision to pursue individual freedom . . . however, they do not have a correspondingly robust vision of social engagement."[11] In order to address this deficiency, the ethics curriculum has been designed to

9. Sharon Daloz Parks, "Is It Too Late? Young Adults and the Formation of Professional Ethics," in *Can Ethics Be Taught? Perspectives, Challenges, and Approaches at Harvard Business School*, ed. Thomas R. Piper, Mary C. Gentile, and Sharon Daloz Parks (Cambridge, Mass.: Harvard Business School, 1993).

10. Ibid., 27.

11. Ibid., 38.

foster "critical-systemic thought" and cultivate understanding of and appreciation for "diverse perspectives."[12]

The goals of the ethics component of the Harvard Business School curriculum correspond to the Social Analysis assignment in advanced field education at Iliff. Despite the previously listed professional formation goals and the prominence of CPE, I contend that cultivating an understanding of contextual and systemic realities is an essential part of ministry preparation and practice. This concern is not new. Ministry is shaped by contextual and social variables as well as individual gifts, skills, and capacities.

With regard to ministry studies at Iliff, individualist assumptions about professional ministry formation have been supplemented with acknowledgment of the importance of social analysis for the understanding and practice of ministry. In the 1980s, some seminaries developed the discipline of Congregational Studies[13] as an important testimony to the importance of understanding context and structural dynamics for the practice of ministry. Rooted in postmodernist assumptions of the importance of context and an appreciation of difference, Congregational Studies provided a needed antidote to the exclusively individualist model that had previously dominated ministry studies. Congregational Studies also drew from the discipline of Organizational Development, which acknowledges that organizations have lives of their own that are more than the individuals that comprise them. As demonstrated in this chapter, this corrective has proven valuable for some students and has been resisted by others. This approach can be particularly affirming for students (especially many students of color) whose starting point is a more communal understanding of selfhood, and it can be particularly challenging for those students, primarily white students, whose first language is individualism.

---

12. Ibid., 52, 53. Parks also found that a predisposition to "robust social engagement" was stronger among students of color and some women than it was among white male students.

13. See James F. Hopewell, *Congregation: Stories and Structures* (Minneapolis: Fortress Press, 1987), and Jackson W. Carroll, Carl S. Dudley, and William McKinney, *Handbook for Congregational Studies* (Nashville: Abingdon Press, 1986).

By the mid 1990s, social analysis had been formally introduced into Iliff's Advanced Field Education curriculum through a fall quarter Social Analysis assignment.[14] In its current form, the Social Analysis assignment consists of four investigations that students undertake in their ministry sites: context; history, people, and space; systems and power; and ethos and theology. In the investigation of context, students walk the neighborhood of their ministry site, interview persons living and working in the neighborhood, examine census data to learn of the area's demographics, and explore the ministry site's relationship with its denomination or professional associations. With regard to history, people, and space, students research the various narratives that shape the site's history, gather data (gender, race, class, age, living conditions, location, etc.) about the congregants/clients/participants, and examine how the physical space the ministry occupies influences what occurs. In the power and systems investigation, students assess both the formal and informal decision making systems, seek to learn who the official and unofficial influencers are, and look into how gender, age, race, length of tenure, etc., affect power dynamics and ways the ministry is organized and functions. In ethos and theology, students give particular attention to how congregants/participants express the meaning of the ministry, which descriptors of meaning dominate, and how congregants/participants both implicitly and explicitly express how or if they understand God to be present, as well as what they believe about human nature and the vocation of the church. In each of the investigations, the student is asked to reflect on what their findings mean both for the practice of ministry in their site and their own professional ministerial formation.

---

14. Attention to context and social location is now common among field education programs in ATS schools although not universal. As a part of my 2007 research on the role of social analysis in field education, I contacted several colleagues in the Association of Theological Field Educators. Although this was not a random sample, seven field educators indicated that their students did little or no social analysis as a part of field education although in most cases they did undertake somewhat similar assignments in required congregational studies courses. Six schools included substantive investigation of context and system dynamics in the field education curriculum.

In 2003, in order to enlarge the students' understanding of the significance of social analysis, the assignment was modified to include group discussion of the various social analysis categories. Previously, each student prepared a paper analyzing her or his site that was presented in the seminar. The nature of the presentations tended to deemphasize analysis and highlight the reporting of facts and observations. The group discussion tended to encourage deeper reflection on what was being discovered and its implications for the practice of ministry. For each of the four investigations, and in preparation for class discussion, students summarized their findings in order to present one or two issues of greatest significance.

Most Iliff students find social analysis valuable for their understanding of ministry.[15] Comments include: "Yes. It is all about context. It is very important to note the social location, the history, the present circumstances, the changes, etc., in determining ministry choices," and "I find this to be extremely helpful as did my placement. This tool can be definitely applicable in any setting."

Other students' evaluative comments not only revealed the importance of social analysis, they also testified to Bellah and his colleagues' observation that individualism is the first language of (dominant culture) American discourse. The comments indicate that social analysis is a "second language" that needs to be learned. One student reflected: "I learned more about a congregation I had been part of for over eight years. I was looking with new lenses in my glasses and saw things I had not seen before."

Others, however, resisted the assignment. In response to a question as to whether social analysis was useful, one student wrote: "Not really. Beyond the fact that paying attention to particulars matters, it isn't at all clear to me how these formalized discussions helped to underscore the specific ways in which context matters." Even after social analysis, some students continued to respond as

---

15. In 2007, I asked 2005–6 and 2006–7 advanced field education students to respond to a questionnaire about their engagement with social analysis in field education. Fourteen of the thirty 2005–6 students and fifteen of the twenty-six 2006–7 students replied to the survey. In addition, I have made use of the student comments about social analysis from fall quarter advanced field education evaluations, which all students were required to submit.

socially unsituated selves. They gained a theoretical understanding of contextual and systemic dynamics, but they remained ensconced in their first language of individualism and saw little if any connection between those dynamics and their practice of ministry.

An important example of how individualism reinforces a lack of connection between social analysis and ministry practice has to do with race and racism.[16] An individualist perspective perpetuates definitions of racism that focus on personal and interpersonal racism to the exclusion of racism's institutional and cultural expressions.[17] Racism is reduced to whether individuals have racist thoughts and/or act prejudicially toward other individuals. If an individual white person is not harboring negative thoughts about persons of color and is not behaving in a racist (prejudicial) manner, then racism does not exist.[18] Racism becomes a matter of whether whites are friendly toward persons of color.[19] An understanding of racism as "a system of advantage based on race"[20] is ignored or rejected, and social/cultural/structural analysis is disregarded when racism is reduced to individual actions. To do otherwise challenges dominant culture assumptions.

An advanced field education student who is white once came to speak with me about her difficulty comprehending the racial tension that existed between her and her supervisor of color.[21] The student told me that she could not help the fact that racism exists; all she

---

16. Factors of gender, sexual orientation, ability, age, etc., similarly could be highlighted as to their importance in understanding the social context and dynamics of ministry.
17. For a helpful summary of how personal, interpersonal, institutional, and cultural racism function in the contemporary context of the United States, see Valerie Batts, *Modern Racism: New Melody for the Same Old Tunes,* EDS Occasional Papers, no. 2 (Cambridge, Mass.: Episcopal Divinity School, 1998).
18. David Wellman, *Portraits of White Racism,* 2nd ed. (New York: Cambridge University Press, 1993). See especially chapter 1, "Prejudiced People Are Not the Only Racists in America."
19. Benjamin DeMott, *The Trouble with Friendship: Why Americans Can't Think Straight about Race* (New York: Grove/Atlantic, 1996).
20. Wellman, *Portraits of White Racism,* 27.
21. The relationship between supervisors and students can never be reduced to a single variable. The dynamics in this particular case were complex. For purposes of highlighting the importance of one aspect of social analysis for deepening ministry formation and practice, I have focused on the role race played.

could do was relate to her supervisor in a "nonracist" manner. I invited the student to think about how racism affected her supervisor, and whether the student had expressed interpersonal racism. The supervisor had to deal with institutional and cultural racism regardless of how she was treated by this student or other individual whites. The student's individual behavior did not change the way the congregation responded to the pastor's leadership or the discrimination to which the pastor was subject in society at large. The student told me that she did not pick up on these issues when she did her social analysis, but that our conversation helped her better understand them. She said that issues of race (and other issues of privilege and oppression) needed more attention in her social analysis and perhaps should be emphasized more in the assignment's instructions. Authentic interactions across racial lines require awareness of institutional and cultural factors as well as intrapsychic and interpersonal ones. Individual cordiality does not erase racism. Social analysis is a preliminary step to the social commitment to dismantle institutional and cultural racism and to developing responses of solidarity and alliance.

The challenge of connecting social analysis with the practice of ministry is further revealed by student responses to questions about the value of social analysis for the two subsequent assignments in the advanced field seminar, a case study in the winter quarter, and the students' theology of ministry paper in the spring. Students found social analysis crucial to their engagement with case studies, writing: "Race, gender, and class were huge in the case study." "I was able to have insight into some of the underlying causes of conflict that I would not have otherwise seen."

However, approximately one-third of the students saw no connection between their social analysis and their case study. Case studies for these students revolved around individual interactions and their analysis assumed that the parties involved were socially unsituated selves.[22] After asking for student responses about the

---

22. Iliff is not alone in facing the challenge of helping students connect social analysis with ministry practice. A field educator at another school observed: "We

connection between their social analysis and their case study, I reviewed the case study assignment and discovered that nothing explicit in the assignment asked students to connect contextual, systemic, structural analysis with their preparation of their case studies. By the way the case study assignment was designed, I was colluding in perpetuating our students' individualism and compartmentalization of knowledge. The revelation resulted in a redesign of the assignment.[23]

Students made even fewer connections between their theology of ministry papers[24] and their social analysis. This suggests a theological understanding that is more individualist than contextual. Students might modify how they express their theology in different contexts, but for most students, context does not shape their theological understandings of their ministry.

Despite the intentions of the Ministry Studies curriculum and program, not all students learn the skills and practices that we try to teach. We have not successfully made the case regarding the importance of the social analysis aspects of the curriculum nor helped all students integrate deeper and more thorough social awareness into their understanding of their professional formation. Some of this is no doubt inevitable. A field educator at another school commented about their Social Analysis assignment: "I can tell you that the success of the process has depended upon the attitudinal disposition of the student." But I do not think we can attribute all responses to individual student attitudes. The gap between the *intentions*

have learned to supervise this assignment energetically because new interns do not understand 'Context' as church ministry as easily as they get 'Worship' or 'Christian Education.' "

23. The previous introduction to the case study assignment stated that a "personal life of faith and spiritual discipline, helping skills of attending, listening, and responding, are the tools of case work." I have now added "careful analysis of the sociocontextual dynamics" to the list of case work tools. I am indebted to my colleague Lynn Rhodes at the Pacific School of Religion, whose comments about social analysis at Pacific School of Religion helped me see connections that can be made between case studies and the Iliff Social Analysis assignment.

24. The Theology of Ministry assignment instructed students to revisit their social analysis. However, the 2007 assignment was modified further to strengthen the connection.

and *outcomes* of the curriculum is something each discipline might productively interrogate.

Concerning social analysis, it will be important to address more directly the dominant culture assumptions about individualism and highlight how social analytical thinking runs counter to the "first language of (dominant culture) American individualism." Some students reported that their understanding of the value of social analysis was deepened after taking the Iliff course, "Congregations: Leadership, Culture and Context." With specific regard to the advanced field education curriculum, strengthening the facilitation of the seminar discussion of the social analysis investigations and making more specific connections with subsequent case study and Theology of Ministry assignments will help students become more fluent in the "second language" of social analysis.

Doing social analysis as a part of ministry formation is not an end in itself. The information gleaned and the understandings achieved demand a response. It is not enough to learn the ways in which context shapes ministry or how power dynamics play out in the system.[25] Holland and Henriot make the distinction between social analysis that is done for purely analytical or "academic" purposes and that which is pastoral or is done for the sake of engaging in more committed and informed social action.[26] Social analysis undertaken as a part of field education and ministerial formation addresses the pastoral dimension. Parks makes a similar point regarding the preparation of socially aware business leaders: "It is not difficult to teach ... ethical systems theory.... The more sobering and challenging task is to develop a curriculum that fosters not only ethical reflection but also the formation of moral courage."[27]

---

25. Occasionally, students have used social analysis not to deepen understanding of how to minister in a particular setting but rather to distance themselves from sites with which they were in conflict. Social analysis undertaken as a part of ministry formation invites the student to ask, "Given the social contexts and structural dynamics, how will I minister here," instead of focusing on "what is wrong with this place."

26. Joe Holland and Peter Henriot, S.J., *Social Analysis: Linking Faith and Justice*, rev. ed. (Maryknoll, N.Y.: Orbis Books, 1983).

27. Parks, "Is It Too Late?" 49.

The practice of social analysis for social justice can be daunting. Ministry is demanding enough when it is limited to accompanying persons as they do their interior work and to helping individuals interact with each other in more loving and compassionate ways. Some students preparing for ministry might understandably shy away from social analysis that calls upon ministers to address systemic issues of equity, justice, privilege, and oppression as well as individual and interpersonal concerns.[28]

In a similar vein, the Social Analysis assignment revealed how insular some congregations and ministries can become. Congregations can become disconnected from their neighborhoods and social locations. Given the needs of congregants and the demands on resources, the impulse to retreat to isolation is not surprising. However, social analysis is not solely for the purpose of extending personal and congregational ministries into the larger arenas of public life. Social analysis also aids in understanding how systems function and in explaining the interrelatedness of individual and systemic dynamics that individualism obscures. One student reported that "the social analysis helped objectify the setting so that I didn't take some things personally whereas I might have done so otherwise." If effectively integrated with personal and interpersonal development, social analysis can complement and strengthen ministry, rather than overwhelm students and ministers with more to do.

## Conclusion

As noted above, advocacy for the use of social analysis to equip students to understand contextual/systemic/structural dynamics should not be taken as a condemnation or devaluing of individuality. Individual freedom is foundational for the free exchange of ideas.

28. A Perkins School of Theology field education assignment requires students to examine causes as well as results: "Observe/reflect on the way the church engages the world.... Examine such things as the church budget; staff assignments; sermons and prayers ... how is the congregation working to deal with causes of injustice, violence, and structural evil?" (excerpted from the Perkins intern assignment "Ministry Contexts: Church and Community").

Individual freedom can be liberating for those who are caught up in oppressive systems. Social analysis not only helps surface the existence of systemic/structural/contextual realities; it also acknowledges them as social constructs rather than essentialist categories. No social setting is isolated from larger national and global contexts, nor is any setting monolithic. There are varieties of subcultures within all ministry settings. Additionally, social systems can be changed through individual initiative for both good and ill.

The advanced field education experience of a female student from Tonga serves as an example of how both individualism and social analysis can contribute positively to social change. Her field placement was in a predominantly white congregation served by a white female senior pastor. The Tongan student's gifts for ministry and capacity for leadership were acknowledged at her field education site in ways they had not been in her home congregation.[29] At her field site, her individual skills and capacities were affirmed, and the malleable nature of church culture was revealed. "It would be a mistake to think of our past and our various social origins as having a fixed or forever unalterable meaning."[30]

Individual development and social analysis and action are not mutually exclusive. Socially aware and personally responsible ministry formation demands both. Such formation can "heighten awareness of the interwoven character of personal and systemic oppression and the importance of keeping an analysis of inner and outer transformation together in liberation ministries."[31]

Because of the influence of individualism in ministry formation, however, the social side of the equation needs greater emphasis than it is often given. Even students who resist reducing all understanding to an individualist perspective will need specific and ongoing work in the "second language" of social analysis in order to deepen

---

29. This is not to say that all Tongan congregations resist female leadership, nor that all white congregations embrace it. In this particular case, however, the student's ability to exercise her individual gifts in a different social context proved valuable for her professional formation.

30. Archie Smith, *The Relational Self: Ethics and Therapy from a Black Church Perspective* (Nashville: Abingdon Press, 1982), 79.

31. Ibid., 14.

and broaden their ministry practice. For dominant culture students, individualism downplays the significance of the "bigger picture" social situation, and it obscures questions of how social location, power dynamics, and systemic advantage and oppression shape large portions of life and work, especially in the United States.

# - 3 -

# Bringing the City to Light

## Pastoral Formation
## in a Multicultural Urban Context

MARTHA R. JACOBS, ELEANOR MOODY-SHEPHERD,
REBECA M. RADILLO

New York Theological Seminary

THE CONTEXT OF metropolitan New York City shapes the community of New York Theological Seminary (NYTS), the more particular context in which we learn, minister, and grow. It is not a community of like minds, backgrounds, geographic birthplaces, denominations, sexual orientations, or even language. It is a people called by God to live as a community bound by Jesus Christ who walk the streets of New York City. We hope that above all else we will come to love our neighbor as we love ourselves. We are called to a radical commitment to inclusiveness and acceptance of the other in this unique location, one of the most diverse cities in the world, and it is out of this social location that we have been called to serve in this broader context.

## Our Context and Student Body

In the early 1990s, NYTS undertook an institutional review and training program that sought to increase the seminary's multicultural awareness and commensurate practices. This project came at a time when globalization was becoming a significant concern for seminaries in North America. A key factor in determining the direction of this endeavor was our realization that globalization and localization were one and the same for us in New York City. Diversity was the norm — on the streets, in our homes, and even in the religious houses of worship in both the city and the surrounding suburbs. Diversity was alive each evening in our classes.

NYTS has been educating men and women of many different races, cultures, languages, social locations, sexual orientations, and national origins in New York City and the tri-state area for over one hundred years. We have students from more than fifty-one denominations from widely diverse racial, ethnic, national, and cultural backgrounds. More than 65 percent of our students are from the African Diaspora. They are straight, lesbian, gay, bisexual, and transgendered, and they represent a wide variety of second- and third-career professionals. They are also prisoners at Sing Sing Correctional Facility where NYTS has had an ongoing Masters of Professional Studies degree program.

As a result of what we learned through this multicultural review and training program,[1] we instituted a new curriculum for the first professional degree, designed and taught new courses, and implemented cultural enrichment activities. We constructed contextual theological education shaped by our unique social location, one of the world's leading centers of commerce and finance, culture and art, education and information. Here, where the neighborhoods are a rich mosaic of people and cultures, and the artistic, civil, political, and religious communities are all part of a vibrant urbanizing and globalizing ethos, we set our focus on the formation of students for ministry in the church and world.

NYTS is a microcosm of this diverse context. It is committed to a formation of its students shaped by a commitment to the transformation of church, city, and world. The question for NYTS reflects the complexity of our location: How do we form fully integrated

---

1. For an assessment of our learning, see Dale T. Irvin, "Open-Ended Pedagogy in a Multicultural Classroom: The Case for Theological Education," *Religious Studies News* 4, no. 1 (February 1996).

persons who become competent ministers for multiracial, multicultural, multilingual urban settings? Where other theological schools are wrestling with the challenge of how to become more diverse, NYTS continues to struggle with the challenge of what it can and must do with the diversity it already experiences. It is here that contextualization is practiced in a different way as we teach and model radical inclusiveness. All are welcome at the NYTS table, even those who resist inclusivity.

## *Contextualization in Practice: Supervised Ministry*

Parker Palmer writes, "Vocation does not mean a goal that I pursue. It means a calling that I hear. Before I can tell my life what I want to do with it, I must listen to my life telling me who I am."[2] We endeavor to help our students listen to what their lives are telling them. We try to ensure that we are not contributing to a fragmented self-understanding while addressing multiculturalism and diversity. These concepts are articulated, grounded, and best exemplified in our Supervised Ministry program, a two-year required curriculum involving at least four areas of ministerial competency: interpretation, performance, contextualization, and formation. The primary goal is to foster a deeper degree of integration of these four competencies. It does so by engaging students, site supervisors, and faculty in a systematic, hands-on action-reflection process based on the actual ministerial experiences of the students who serve in multicultural urban churches, hospitals, nonprofit, and social service agencies. Once a month students meet in a "safe space" to reflect in small groups with a group leader. That leader is intentional in ensuring that students engage in the process of critical reflection and praxis, each equally significant to the process. It is essential that students understand the contextual issues that arise at their sites. Supervised Ministry challenges students by placing them in

---

2. Parker Palmer, *Let Your Life Speak: Listening for the Voice of Vocation* (San Francisco: Jossey-Bass, 1999), 4.

sites that are new to their experience and that call on new or refined skills.

Over the course of these four semesters, most of the students are transformed. They come to realize that ministry is always done in a particular context, never in a vacuum. This part of their education forms practical, responsible, and ethical guidelines for ministry that are rooted in an understanding of human agency and identity defined by healing and transformation in a holistic fashion. It is hoped that they become "increasingly aware of the contextual content of a text or setting in which they find themselves, so that they might be more attuned to their own cultural and religious biases and the effects of those biases in their ministry, whether in congregations or elsewhere."[3]

The crux of the Supervised Ministry program is formation through the integration of cognition and praxis that leads to pastoral competence and the emergence of ministerial identity. The framework for this integrative process is informed by the work of Wiggins and McTigue's model for how "a faculty might visualize its understanding of integrative process."[4]

There are six key aspects identified as critical in the process of understanding and integration. Each aspect poses several questions that engage seminarians in critical reflection that subsequently results in their raising questions of meaning. The outcome of this critical reflection and the raising of questions of meaning results in clarity of action in response to particular situations in ministry.

For NYTS contextualization is an ongoing process, at the core of which is authentic hospitality and healthy diversity. Contextualization calls into question "absolutes." It allows for a multiplicity of meaning-making experiences. It expands the interpretation of every aspect of theological education through critical thinking and praxis.

---

3. Charles R. Foster, Lisa E. Dahill, Lawrence A. Golemon, and Barbara Wang Tolentino, *Educating Clergy: Teaching Practices and Pastoral Imagination* (San Francisco: Jossey-Bass, 2006), 138.

4. Victor J. Klimoski, Kevin O'Neill, and Katrina Schuth, eds., *Educating Leaders for Ministry: Issues and Responses* (Collegeville, Minn.: Liturgical Press, 2005), 70–71.

One of the founding tenets of NYTS is the conviction that men and women from different faith traditions can study the Bible and prepare to serve their communities of faith together. We are convinced that "every religion, no matter what we may understand by *religion,* is a situated reality in a specific human context, a concrete and determined geographical space, historical moment and social milieu."[5] Therefore, being intentional about helping students better understand their religion while also understanding the religious traditions of others is central to our contextual education process. They can "become aware of the unexamined assumptions of their religious tradition and practice."[6]

Contextualization is intentionally addressed in every course. It calls the faculty into accountability, and it is one of the foundations upon which the NYTS curriculum is built. In order to remain effective, contextualization demands an ongoing educational process on the part of educators as well as a dialogical engagement with the different contexts in which they interact.

Contextualization is rooted in "a bio-psycho-social-spiritual conceptual model,"[7] which gives a clear and visual way to understand these four major aspects of a seminarian's personal development. This model provides a foundation for the process of formation. As Rebeca Radillo writes, "The interplay between the cognitive and practical implications of contextualized education fosters the unfolding as authentic pastors/leaders and as true agents of transformation in a very difficult and complex context."[8]

Our pedagogy seeks "to help students become attuned to their own culture, bias, ministry style, and background as they do social analysis . . . while learning to . . . exegete texts from a feminist,

---

5. Otto Maduro, *Religion and Social Conflicts* (Maryknoll, N.Y.: Orbis Books, 1982), 41.

6. Foster et al., *Educating Clergy,* 136.

7. Rebeca Radillo, "A Model of Formation in the Multi-cultural Urban Context for the Pastoral Care Specialist," Sect. II, in *The Formation of Pastoral Counselors: Challenges and Opportunities,* ed. Duane R. Bidwell and Joretta L. Marshall (Binghamton, N.Y.: Haworth Press, 2007), 175.

8. Ibid.

womanist, or mujerista perspective."[9] Additionally, students are introduced to liberation, progressive and transformative perspectives of exegesis and social analysis. Becoming more aware of the "other" enables students to develop the capacity to "hear each other out of the experience of the other, toward some reconciling action with each other and the groups they represent."[10]

We are called to be a part of a diverse community as we strive to understand one another and to be in a community of shared difference.[11] Being in community requires that we be in open dialogue in order to have an authentic conversation that enables us to understand others. Humberto Alfaro, a professor at NYTS, commented: "An authentic 'conversation' is possible only when the two parties are committed to 'mutual transformation' based on a shared commitment for more justice, equality, and peace. When there is no desire, intention, or passion for knowing one another and for moving toward a wider world, what value is there to any 'conversation'?"[12] As Yvette Flunder reminds us, "When the stories begin to flow out of one experience to another, and from one person to another, similarities begin to emerge around which people can identify and community forms."[13]

## The Hermeneutical Inventory

Seminarians reflect the mix of influences that have shaped their biblical understanding and worldview. Hence, the first year of study is designed to help them develop skills and insights that they can

9. Foster, *Educating Clergy*, 132–33.

10. Ibid.

11. Lester Edwin J. Ruiz, "Radical Inclusion: The Purpose of Cartography as Grand Theorizing." This essay is a slightly revised excerpt from his "After Grand Theory: Pilgrim-Pirates of the Earth and the Limits and Possibilities of Radical Inclusion — Conversations along the Way to Peace, Security and Conviviality" presented at an international seminar entitled "Towards a Grand Theory of Peace: Peace, Security, and Conviviality after 9/11," sponsored by International Christian University, Tokyo, June 1–6, 2007.

12. Ibid., 10.

13. Yvette Flunder, *Where the Edge Gathers: Building a Community of Radical Inclusion* (Cleveland: Pilgrim Press, 2005), 11.

use to critique their own theological, political, and social locations. When they become more aware of the factors at work in their own historical experiences that shaped their biblical understanding, they are better able to understand and appreciate the perspectives of the others. Therefore, all first-year students complete a hermeneutical inventory that asks them twenty probing questions, including:

+ What are the norms or standards beyond the Bible recognized in my tradition to indicate how and in what particulars the Bible is the Word of God?

+ What is my actual working theology regarding interpretation of the Bible? To what extent is this the same or different from the official position of my denomination or the "average" viewpoint among my church associates?

+ Is my working theology more or less the same as my formal theology, such as I might state in an application to a seminary or before a church body?

+ How do my ethnic or 'racial' history, culture, and consciousness influence my interpretation of the Bible? (The same question is asked about gender, orientation, and social class.)

+ Have I experienced crises in my life in which the Bible was a resource or in which I came to a deeper or different understanding of the Bible than I had held before? If so, what has been the lasting effect of the crisis on my biblical interpretation?

+ What has been my experience of spiritual awareness or guidance from God in interpreting the Bible?

+ What language or images express my spiritual awareness or guidance in interpreting the Bible?

+ Do I have a "spiritual" way of using or interpreting the Bible that is different from other ways I might read or interpret the Bible?

+ Do these different approaches to the Bible combine comfortably for me, or are they in tension or conflict?

After completing the inventory, the reflecting process includes the following questions:

- ◆ What new awareness do I gain from this self-inventory as to how I actually interpret the Bible?

- ◆ What more do I want to learn about the workings of some of these hermeneutical factors in my biblical interpretation?

- ◆ What may I want to consider changing in my attitude or practice that I may become a more adequate and self-consistent biblical interpreter?

The inventory "helps students see ancient texts, events, and traditions in their own context; to extricate their original meanings from the layers of meaning that have accrued to them over the centuries."[14] Further, it is intended to raise their "awareness and appreciation for diversity in the human experience,"[15] while ensuring that cultural, social, and economic perspectives are examined and critiqued.

Rebeca Radillo reminds us that the process of formation is not uniform, but rather depends on individual persons in their particular milieus. To think otherwise, "results in processes that are exclusive and individualistic, ignoring or diminishing the importance of contextual realities. To disregard the social, biological, and spiritual forces that from birth have been at work in the lives of persons leads to a partial or fragmented self-understanding."[16]

## Conclusion

Contextualization at New York Theological Seminary is complex given the diverse student body, a wide denominational representation, a myriad of sociological, political, historical, and economic backgrounds, and the multicultural metropolitan context of New

---

14. Foster, *Educating Clergy*, 137.
15. Ibid., 143.
16. Radillo, "A Model of Formation in the Multi-cultural Urban Context for the Pastoral Care Specialist," 168.

York City. It is at this juncture where the work of inclusion becomes critical in the ongoing methodological and pedagogical tasks that will take the seminary into the future.

Pedagogies of contextualization are a prominent component in the NYTS classroom, but most intentionally with Supervised Ministry. We have sought to provide what Foster calls "contextual transformation."[17] We endeavor to "equip students with the knowledge, skills, and sensibilities for critical reflection and action in the classroom to take up the challenge of transforming the structures of racism, oppression or marginalization"[18] — and we would add sexism, classism, heterosexism, and denominationalism.

---

17. Foster, *Educating Clergy,* 151.
18. Ibid., 152.

# – 4 –

# Intercultural Immersions within Contextual Education

## JOSEPH S. TORTORICI

### Wesley Theological Seminary

*My sensitivity and awareness of other cultures has increased
. . . as well as my desire to inquire and learn more and be genuinely interested in those who cross my path. It has flowed
into my preaching, teaching, leading of worship, and into my
service and leading in mission projects.*   —Wesley Graduate

**W**ESLEY THEOLOGICAL SEMINARY, along with many other
seminaries, sees intercultural immersion experiences as an
effective educational method for students to deepen their self-
understanding as cultural persons. This education is transforma-
tional when students become aware of the limitations of their own
culture, integrate this awareness into a new self-understanding, and
then make informed choices based on the integrated information.
Most students who participate in immersions are more confident
in reaching out to other cultural groups, whether it is simply to
become acquainted, to invite others into worship participation, or
to become involved in a specific local ministry. Because church leaders today must be savvy about the global village in which we live,
these immersion experiences prepare students for ministry where,
even within rural settings, globalizing forces and new immigrant
communities are impacting the economic, cultural, and social fabric
of life.

## *Wesley's Intercultural Immersion*

The intercultural immersion requirement at Wesley Theological
Seminary is one of four components of a comprehensive ministerial
formation program titled Practice in Ministry and Mission (PMM).
In 1993, Wesley launched PMM as a pilot program to replace its
traditional field education program. It was a clear move to meet the
experiential learning needs of the growing student body through an
integrated "contextual education" program. The program was fully
adopted in 1996. The three additional components of the PMM program are pastoral internships, Covenant Discipleship groups, and
theological reflection seminars.

In the decade since its inception, more than 650 Wesley graduates have been "immersed" in cultures different from their own —
from Appalachia to Zimbabwe. Students and faculty have met and
engaged in dialogue with people on every continent, where relationships have been formed with churches, governments, and individuals. They have been introduced to the aftermath of apartheid in
South Africa, the ravages of AIDS in several African nations, and
the devastating effects of mountaintop coal removal in Appalachia.
Students have walked through the Auschwitz concentration camp
in Poland, the Adobe Indian Pueblos of New Mexico, and the
conflicted Mexican/U.S. border communities of Nogales. Institutional relationships have been established with seminaries in Korea,
China, Russia, and Zimbabwe. Wesley students and faculty have
been enriched by the immersion experience and have shared significant learnings with the seminary community, their churches, their
communities, and their families.

In the world of intercultural studies, Wesley's program is seen as a
short-term intercultural program. Longer-term immersions are usually associated with university semester or year-long study abroad
programs. Recent research[1] has understood how short-term programs of two or three weeks, properly organized and with attention

---

1. Janet Hulstrand, "Education Abroad on the Fast Track," *International
Educator* (May–June 2006): 46–55.

to opportunities for deep reflection during the immersion, can have significant impact on the lives of students.

While participating in an intercultural immersion, students are participant-observers. They learn by firsthand observation. The nature of the interactive process of the immersion can also open students to seeing themselves from the perspective of another culture. This heightened awareness contributes to learning more about who they are as persons and as Christians in a global context. In a variety of ways, Wesley graduates express their gratitude for the immersion experience by naming these values inherent in the opportunity: to experience another culture through participation and observation; to reflect theologically upon their daily experiences; to experience the work of God in the lives of other people; and to learn more about themselves and their own culture.

## *The Research*

One goal of the intercultural immersion is for students to experience a personal transformation that increases their cultural competency and enables them to work in varied ministry contexts. Is this goal met? Is this in fact the experience of students? Do they experience transformation as a result of participation in an intercultural immersion? Does this transformation translate into students acquiring competencies for leadership in multicultural contexts? Does this result in more effective ministry? To explore these questions, Wesley master of arts and master of divinity graduates and Association of Theological School (ATS) faculty at thirty-four seminaries participated in a two-pronged research project of surveys and interviews.[2] Both survey and interview data reveal that the immersion is indeed a significant experience for most students and has long-lasting impact on the lives of the participants. For example, when asked to describe their immersion experience, 47 percent of graduates responded that

---

2. The research project cited here was conducted as part of a sabbatical leave with the research assistance of Shenandoah Gale, M.A., M.T.S., a graduate of Wesley Theological Seminary. Her study of Jack Mezirow's work on cognitive transformation provided one of the theoretical frameworks for the research study.

it was "a highlight of my seminary studies"; 65 percent indicated that it sensitized them to another culture; and 44 percent responded that "it was a life-changing experience." In addition, the opportunity to address prejudices and stereotypes and to see the world and the church as others do was a valued challenge. As one graduate said, "I had to set aside a set of lenses through which I viewed the church and the world and learn to observe at a more basic level, to defer conclusions in the interest of just taking in images, and to let those images reveal the truth at the core of the experience." Again and again, graduates expressed that the immersion transformed them as individuals, and as a result it shaped their approach to ministry. In fact, 88 percent of Wesley graduates interviewed described their immersion as transformative.

## *Transformation*

The work of adult education theorist Jack Mezirow was used in this study to address the phenomenon of transformation. Mezirow examines the process by which adults transform their worldview as a result of a learning experience, such as intercultural immersion. Transformation is a shift in perspective whereby persons become critically aware of the limitations of their worldview and as a result expand this worldview.[3]

The intercultural immersion is a learning experience that offers students the opportunity to "transform problematic frames of reference — sets of fixed assumptions and expectations... to make them more inclusive, discriminating, open, reflective, and emotionally able to change."[4] Responses from fifteen of the eighteen graduates interviewed concur that the immersion had such an effect. Thirteen graduates affirmed that the transformation has continued throughout their ministry. Graduates also described their experience as challenging: "A hugely different experience from anything else I

---

3. Jack Mezirow and Associates, *Learning as Transformation: Critical Perspectives on a Theory in Progress* (San Francisco: Jossey-Bass, 2000), 19.
4. Jack Mezirow and Associates, "Transformative Learning as Discourse," *Journal of Transformative Education* 1, no. 1 (2003): 58–63.

had ever encountered"; "it was just so not what I was expecting, it was such a surprise"; it was "eye-opening," and "mind-blowing." Wesley alumni responded that the short-term intercultural immersion served as an initial stage of transformation. Mezirow names this initial experience as a "disorienting dilemma" in which the immersion context reveals to students that their worldview shaped by their context of origin is too limited to interpret the immersion culture. This disorientation is an opportunity to reconsider these newly illuminated assumptions. One graduate stated, "I think we all discovered that parts of us that we had failed to admit to or recognize were uncovered in the immersion. The change was overcoming, as we experienced others overcoming barriers — seeing the person and not the stereotype." Another graduate shared, the immersion "reinforced my understanding of how much of who I am is shaped by my cultural background and environment. I was reminded that there are lots of ways of living life and my way isn't the only way or the right way."

Critically reflecting on our worldview and integrating this new, broader perspective are next steps in the transformation process. The following graduate's reflection illustrates how integrating critical reflection informs daily life. This graduate participated in the deaf culture immersion at the Gallaudet School for the Deaf.

> We have a new puppy and my dog walker is not only a Gallaudet graduate and deaf, but she is in a wheelchair. I don't think I would have hired her had I not been on this program. I think I would have thought, 'I'm a very sensitive person, and I'm trying to be inclusive, but there are twelve steps to my front door and Dalmatians are very active, particularly puppies. How can this work with someone who is extremely hard of hearing and has to get up and down the steps? . . . This is not going to work.' I don't think I would have followed through . . . without this class [immersion]. I would not have pursued the recommendation that she is a wonderful dog walker, and I would not have considered it to be prejudice or discrimination. I would have considered it practical.

Wesley supports the process of transformation from lesser to greater cultural competency once students return from the immersion experience. The integration of new skills is supported by an immersion orientation and debriefing, post-immersion chapel service, professors encouraging students to integrate the immersion experience into course content, and presentations to church groups and the seminary community. The following story illustrates transformation from the immersion experience and the consequent application and integration of a broader worldview into the ministry setting.

> Where I was raised, parents would be considered a failure if their children did not move out — and usually move out of town. The sign that you've been a successful parent is that your children leave. That's not true in southern Appalachia. It's quite common for children to be building houses or living in a trailer on the edge of their parents' property and raising their families there. So you have these close-knit communities. And at the time it was just an interesting cultural observation, 'Oh, this is just different than the way I grew up.' I'm now serving in a church where I have people who have come from all over the area, but I also have some old Maryland families that are rooted in the western Appalachia parts of Maryland who have kids still living at home, and they are thirty. And it's that insight that I got on the trip that has enabled me to look at those families without judging them as parental failures. This is a difference that they are very comfortable with, and they see it as their family being close knit.

Other alumni were briefer in their indication of how their immersion experience has transformed their practice of daily ministry:

> Inclusiveness has become important to me, and I continually work to bring everyone to the table. I look for the differences in the congregation and invite persons of various cultures to contribute to our worship.

I've learned to watch, wait, and observe without judging people. [The immersion] helped me to discover more about the meaning and values of people's behaviors.

On my immersion I learned new forms of prayer, outside of my tradition, and have introduced them into our regular worship services creating a more contemplative atmosphere.

One beneficial consequence of an immersion experience is a new sensitivity to stereotypes, racially injurious references, and prejudicial attitudes present in the American culture. Students who grew in such sensitivity reported working at making changes in their own language and viewpoints, as well as working to bring about shifts in the perspectives of those whom they serve. For instance, the yearly immersion in the culture of the deaf often leads to action for change. In several instances, students who had completed their immersion among the deaf returned home to challenge their church communities and leaders to open their doors to the deaf and initiate new ministries of pastoral care to those in the deaf community. In these cases, what started as an individual transformation developed into community transformation.

Wesley's intercultural immersion is an opportunity for seminary students to examine, reconsider, and transform their perspectives about themselves and the world so that upon serving the church they may continue to be open to other cultural views and open to acquiring competencies not previously possessed.

## *Intercultural Competency*

Intercultural competencies are the skills, attitudes, and behaviors that enable us to be effective in our ministry across cultural contexts. Intercultural immersions offer seminary students an opportunity to expand limited worldviews. The expansion of a student's worldview prepares a student to be more open to engaging a wider range of capacities.

In response to the survey question, "Did your intercultural immersion experience contribute to your competency in ministering to persons of other cultures?" 62 percent responded *yes.* Words such as *sensitivity, awareness, openness, understanding, confidence, compassion, empathy,* and *perspective* were often used to describe the positive influence of their immersion experience. For example, the immersion "helped me communicate with other cultures and be a better listener"; "increased my ability to see the world as others see it"; "helped me personalize a culture"; "helped me be more confident in reaching out to other cultures"; and "increased my objectivity about people."

What kinds of competency skills are helpful for intercultural situations? The competency area Wesley graduates considered most important for being effective in intercultural ministry is that of *attitude.* Having an attitude of openness to people from other cultures, while possessing a respect for and acceptance of differences, were the ones most often named by students. As one graduate stated, "the skill most needed is openness. We are all too quick to judge people who don't do things the way we do. It limits God's grace." Awareness of one's own culture, awareness of other people's culture, and awareness of how cultures interact is fundamental to effective ministry in multicultural contexts. "Being willing to listen to the needs of the person — listening with some consciousness of one's own cultural prejudices, your body language, words you choose, facial expressions — whether it's the homeless population or newly arrived immigrant. We need to recognize the differences."

*Knowledge* of another's culture is also fundamental for engendering respect for that culture. The ability to listen, observe, and more openly interpret others' behavior are basic *skills* in any ministry, and all the more so when trying to effectively pastor within an intercultural context with varied languages, values, nonverbal behaviors, traditions, and customs. One student reflected, "I think the big one is stopping to listen to what something means to people from their own perspective instead of rushing in to interpret it from my perspective." Given that there are cultural differences and perspectives among peoples, it is important to "learn to wait and see what something means for another person."

In the real estate world, the maxim is "location, location, location." In ministry we can say it is "context, context, context." Understanding the context of the people among whom we minister is crucial to being an effective pastor. A recent graduate put it this way: "I came from a military culture, and it's quite different from where I am now. I am pastoring in a small town.... It took me a long time to understand that the place where I'm serving is a kind of 'folk culture.' I think you need to discern what kind of culture you are ministering in and what of the Gospel is relevant in that setting. And it's not something I ever thought. I thought I was going to a United Methodist church, and that's the way it is."

Immersions can engender in students particular attitudes, knowledge, and skills for ministry with people across cultures. In the research interview, one ATS faculty member gave the following example.

> One year when I went on an immersion with students, a couple who had a commitment to a simplified lifestyle came back from the immersion with their commitments deepened. ...[One] student since graduation has continued [his commitment]. In our denomination, he is the chair of the Social Justice Commission. I believe his immersion experience helped to equip him for the role of leadership for this commission. It deepened his sensibility to the work of this commission.

Students may also develop the attitude for a new or increased capacity to feel empathy and compassion for others. Another ATS faculty member reported that after an immersion in Indonesia he noticed a common theme in the student papers.

> They would never look at the Islamic religion the same. They slept at mosques. They mingled with Muslims and came to understand they were highly intelligent, religious, and not terrorists. One of the comments made by a student was that whenever any difficulty or disaster occurs in that part of the world, they will always be emotionally connected to that people, because they have become their people as well.

## Immersions in
## Other Seminary Settings

To determine if and how other ATS seminaries conduct intercultural immersions, we surveyed seminary faculty at 134 schools and were able to interview faculty at 19 of these schools. We found that intercultural immersion experiences have increasingly become part of seminary curriculum among members of the Association of Theological Schools. While one ATS seminary has had an immersion requirement since the founding of the seminary in 1947, it is only since the early 1970s that the majority of immersion programs have come into existence. The increase in programs was a response to globalization and the challenge for the church to address the growing diversity of cultures represented in their congregations and ministry contexts. Of the initial 134 seminaries surveyed, 89 reported having immersions as a requirement or an elective, or having a special program of studies addressing intercultural experiential education. The goal of these immersion programs is to provide adequate and appropriate preparation for ministry and mission within a many-cultured global reality.

Resources for implementing intercultural immersion programs vary from seminary to seminary. The majority requires students to fund their immersions "out of pocket" as well as take advantage of minimal scholarship funds. Some seminaries have endowments and scholarship funds that enable students to take advantage of expensive international immersion trips. One advantage for all of the seminaries studied is that seminary faculty lead the majority of the immersion trips. This enables faculty and students to engage in the immersion with a common understanding of the experience, which is rooted in the values and mission of the seminary culture. The sharing of the immersion experiences in this way has the possibility of future integration into the seminary curriculum. ATS faculty interviewed reported similar stories of transformation through immersion leading to increased cultural competency.

## Conclusion

Wesley graduates and ATS faculty give evidence that immersions are a vital part of seminary training in our current global reality. Through transformation of their own worldviews, students are more open to learning the competencies necessary to minister effectively with individuals and communities of different cultures. Intercultural programs such as Wesley's are gradually becoming a standard component of curricula in North American seminaries. Immersions are called by different names, but the common goal is to intentionally prepare students for ministry and mission in a multicultural global reality. Many Wesley graduates who participated in an intercultural immersion experienced a transformation in perspective, and they acquired, if not cultural competencies for ministry, at least recognition of the knowledge, skills, and attitudes needed for ministry among people across cultures. The intercultural immersion experience and the global connections formed by students and seminaries throughout the world are transforming the face of theological education and, hopefully, the effectiveness of church leaders ministering in today's global reality.

# – 5 –

# An Ethic of Risk
# at the School of the Prophets

VIKI MATSON

Vanderbilt Divinity School

THE POET ADRIENNE RICH dares to assume that age after age, with no extraordinary power, we can reconstitute the world.[1] The writer of the book of Revelation envisions a similar dream of a new heaven and a new earth, but claims that it will come about through the *extra*-ordinary means of divine intervention (21:1–4). No matter how change comes about, whether it is human agency, divine will, or a divine-human partnership, at Vanderbilt Divinity School we believe that what we do can help heal the world. This bold claim gives definition to every aspect of our school, including Field Education.

I begin this reflection from the vantage point of a Global Positioning System. We see the dot of Vanderbilt Divinity School, and we see that it is situated in the American South: the land of the civil War, the civil rights movement, Elvis, Flannery O'Connor, mountain religion and big city cathedrals, Will Campbell and George Wallace, the Ku Klux Klan, Hurricane Katrina. It is a land of mostly red states, bluegrass, and an occasional yellow-dog Democrat. We zoom in a little more, and we see that Vanderbilt Divinity School is situated in the heart of Nashville: a city where college students from Fisk

---

1. Adrienne Rich, "Natural Resources" in *The Dream of a Common Language* (New York: W. W. Norton, 1978).

University and Vanderbilt organized lunchcounter protests; a city where Johnny Cash found his voice; a city brimming with immigrants from Mexico and Latin America, Africa and Kurdistan; a city of prophetic black preachers, storefront ministries, mainline congregations, and a Hindu temple in a western suburb. Zoom in even closer on the neighborhood of Vanderbilt Divinity School, and we see that it is part of a larger university: an elite, conservative, largely white university that was founded with money from a ship mogul with a checkered past; a university on the edge of downtown, abutting the creativity and commerce of Music Row and bordered on another side by government housing projects. Within this garden campus the GPS flags a law school, a medical school, a school of business, a nursing school, a losing football team, an undergraduate student body with a serious drinking problem, a freshman who allegedly committed a hate crime against a gay man, a Greek culture, and a liberal divinity school. We zoom closer to the very life of Vanderbilt Divinity School, but it cannot be viewed fully from the GPS. And so questions remain. What is this school about? Who do we say that we are?

A defining moment in our school's life came in 1960, when the faculty faced a crucial, ethical decision that would affect their own futures. That decision concerned James Lawson, a young African American man who traveled south from Ohio to participate in the civil rights struggle. He was employed by the Fellowship for Reconciliation as the southern field director and assigned to Nashville. His first task was to organize and teach people methods of nonviolent resistance. A few months into his stay, he entered the divinity school as one of the first African Americans admitted to Vanderbilt. In the spring semester, he was arrested for his participation in a sit-in with other students at one of Nashville's downtown restaurants. When the chancellor of the university heard about the arrest, he suspended Lawson from Vanderbilt. During the following summer months, the faculty of the divinity school petitioned the chancellor for Lawson's readmittance. As the summer drew to a close, the chancellor still had not changed his decision, and it became clear that the divinity school faculty had to take more drastic measures. They resigned en masse. In response to this risky act, the chancellor refused to accept the resignations of the divinity school faculty and readmitted Lawson. It was a courageous moment that half a century later still gives definition to who we are as Vanderbilt Divinity School.

As a result of this region-shaking event, the faculty wrote the mission statement that currently defines our school. Within this mission statement are four "commitments" that serve as our moral compass. We embody the challenge and promise of each commitment as we revise curricula, invite guest lecturers, enroll students, and hire new faculty. These four commitments are:

1. The school is committed to do all in its power to combat the idolatry of racism and ethnocentrism which remains widespread in our society.

2. The school is committed to opposing the sexism that has characterized much of the history of the church and is still present in our society.

3. The school is committed to confronting the homophobia that prevails throughout much of the church and society.

4. The school is committed to a program of theological education that is open to and takes account of the religious pluralism in our world.

These commitments are featured prominently in our catalog and in recruiting materials. We refer to them often when discussing the character of our school. We appeal to them when we sense some of the faculty wanting to retrench or take us in a "safer" direction. These commitments appear in our convocation addresses, our sermons, our prayers, our pitches to prospective students. They represent an authoritative text for our school that serves as a constant reminder of who we are.

In addition to the James Lawson affair and our four commitments, there is an architectural artifact in our courtyard that serves as a powerful reminder of our identity. This artifact is an eight-foot granite lintel saved from the ashes of the fire of 1932 in which Wesley Hall, the original building of what was then called the School of the Bible, was destroyed. Carved into that lintel is the Latin phrase *Schola Prophetorum:* School of the Prophets. Every day, as we enter the Divinity School to work or to study, we are reminded of who we are, *a School of the Prophets.* It is the stuff of legend and student T-shirts and meaningful baccalaureate addresses. It is the essence of our identity.

In light of these three dimensions of our school's life — the James Lawson event, our public commitments, and the granite lintel in our courtyard — we believe that we are situated to educate religious leaders with strong social justice inclinations. We are poised to cultivate in our students an impulse to be agents for social justice, to address lingering social ills in their own practice of religious leadership, and to be a progressive religious voice in a culture in which most religious leaders (even in our own neighborhood, city, and region) are singing in a very different key. As field educators, we are famous for telling our students that *context matters,* and we submit that our unique context at Vanderbilt gives definition and energy to our work of preparing our students with the capacities required for progressive religious leadership in our times.

Progressive religious leadership, as we understand it, takes many different shapes. It is known in the work of two divinity students who noticed that rape victims were not being adequately cared for among local pastoral care circles, and so they established the Rape and Sexual Abuse Center. It is found in the Sunday liturgy at a black church whose pastor decided that the issue of HIV/AIDS would be named every Sunday for one year (fifty-two Sundays), whether in prayers, in litanies, or in the sermon. It is experienced in the white United Methodist congregation that put a moratorium on weddings in their sanctuary stating that "until ALL people in committed relationships can get married here, no one will be married here."

Many qualities and gifts are needed for such leadership, but primarily what is required is the capacity to take risks — such as speaking truth to power, communicating an unpopular message, standing in solidarity with those on the margins. Religious leadership in these times requires the intellectual, personal, spiritual, and moral resources to take wise and calculated risks, not for the sake of risk itself, but toward the end of reconstituting the world, or, if I may be so bold to claim, bringing about a New Earth.

As field educators, we believe that our practices reveal theological commitments. I want to suggest that the notion of risk is a profoundly theological one, and I want to propose some places we might mine as we think theologically about risk.

The notion of risk has many theological roots and supports. In Scripture we find Abraham and Sarah, risking it all to honor a divine nudging. We find Moses, perhaps the first human *coyote*, risking the lives of his people to lead them across borders into a more promising land.

We find the Hebrew prophets with an uncompromisingly clear-eyed vision of what the New Earth could look like. And, of course, we find Jesus, whose ministry was characterized by risk for the sake of a new realm, a new way of being together. Even the history of his followers reveals story after story of risk-takers. From Martin Luther to Walter Rauschenbusch to Martin Luther King to Desmond Tutu, we see people willing to risk everything in order to transform the world.

Yet, while Scripture and history reveal deep commitments to an ethic of risk-taking, I want to reflect on one theological category that often promotes contentment rather than risk and suggest another interpretation that informs our preparation of progressive religious leaders. That theological category is pneumatology, the theology of the Holy Spirit.

Traditionally, the Holy Spirit has been understood by such metaphors as Comforter, Counselor, and Advocate. Our experience of the Holy Spirit often has been associated with mystical, even ecstatic individual religious experiences. We speak of the "indwelling of the Holy Spirit," or being "filled with" the Holy Spirit — metaphors that imply being inhabited by or satiated with the presence of God. One interpretation of Galatians claims that if we are *filled with the Spirit*, then our lives will bear fruits, and we will be known by certain virtues or qualities. While surely the case could be made that a life marked by kindness, gentleness, and long-suffering could compel a person to engage in a ministry characterized by risk, I suggest that more often than not the opposite is true — that being *filled with* is accompanied by postures of contentment and comfort. One could compare it to the feeling of being full after a good meal. Contentment rarely prompts risk.

I submit that these images of the Holy Spirit work against an ethic of risk. They reinforce a posture of being satisfied with current realities. The center becomes safe and comfortable and the Holy Spirit's role is to knit our hearts together. Churches, divinity schools, small groups, and institutions that live out of a "safe pneumatology" rarely have language about changing the world in their mission statement. They do not, for example, take risks with liturgical language, or with embracing neighbors who speak another language, or with ordaining women or gay ministers. Instead, the warmth of community is a higher value.

A contrasting view of Spirit can be found in Luke's Gospel. With a reference to Isaiah, Luke quotes Jesus saying, "The spirit of the Lord is *upon me* ... therefore he has anointed me to preach good news to the poor, to proclaim freedom to the captives, restore sight to the blind and free the oppressed" (Luke 4:18–19). I suggest that this spatial shift — from *being filled with* to *being upon me* might be accompanied by a shift in one's sense of responsibility for repairing the world. Experiencing spirit as *upon me* like a weight, a conscience, a goad, or a burden could make one more inclined to take risks for the sake of the Gospel. Then it might be true that risk-takers experience the flames of Pentecost more like a *slow burn* that keeps prodding a life toward justice than like a blazing campfire by which we are all warmed. The spirit of the Lord is *upon me* to bring good news to the poor, etc. When the spirit leans on us like a moral weight, when this "pneumatological burn" works on us over time, it could lend courage and immediacy to our actions.

Such theological reframing undergirds our practice of ministry in field education as we strive to prepare religious leaders unafraid to take risks for the transformation of the world. In light of this foundation, Vanderbilt does some things every well. For instance, we develop field placements that require a tremendous amount of risk on the part of the student. We are careful that our preparations will make their experience successful, but the element of risk exists. For instance, after a trip to the United States–Mexico border through Border Links, two students wanted to intern with a faith-based group in Middle Tennessee that works with immigrants and farm workers. We quickly discovered that there is no such agency in our area, and so we challenged the students to create one. A local justice center agreed to host them. We recruited three seasoned and gifted supervisors to assist them, and we let their field education internship be the work of starting this new organization. Happily, it was a wonderful year. There now is a faith-based group in Middle Tennessee that works with immigration issues and farm worker rights called *Strangers No Longer,* and they are presently in the process of seeking 501(c)3 status. Because we have such a broad understanding of ministry, we are able to match a student's real passion with grassroots justice efforts, even if these efforts are only a dream in someone's imagination.

We also put our students in proximity with risk-takers in our community. We cultivate them as Field Education supervisors. We invite them to preach in our chapel. We host them at our informal brown bag events where they talk about their ministry. Every other year, we teach an experiential "Church in the City" course in which we walk around our city, observe urban ministry up close, and encounter many of the risk-takers along the way.

We do many things well as we promote an ethic of risk with our students; however, there are some things we could do better. We could do better about asking our students to intentionally reflect on the risk-taking dimension of their ministry at their internship. We could do better at helping students understand the moments of risk in every placement. We could talk more about this as a faculty. We could be more intentional about the ways we model risk-taking in our teaching. We can always do better. That is why it is so important to remember who we are when we walk onto the campus of Vanderbilt Divinity School each day. We are a School of the Prophets.

Poets should have the first and last word, so I will end with the conviction Adrienne Rich extols: that with no extraordinary power we can indeed reconstitute the world.[2]

---

2. Rich, "Natural Resources."

# – 6 –

# Teaching Congregations Initiative

## A Paradigm for Forming Church Leaders in Mission-Shaped Communities

### H. STANLEY WOOD

### San Francisco Theological Seminary

T HE FOCUS OF San Francisco Theological Seminary (SFTS) is "Preparing Whole Leaders for the Whole Church" through the intentional integration of skills and arts of ministry, spiritual formation, and critical theological reflection. SFTS is unique among seminaries of the Presbyterian Church (USA) in that all M.Div. graduates are required to participate in internships equivalent in duration to an academic year. These internships are a key component of our integrative learning, and they may be done during summers, in part-time weekends during the school year, or as full-time ministry commitments prior to the last year of academic studies.

The Teaching Congregation Initiative is the intentional matching of our students with mission-shaped communities (internship sites) that are healthy[1] and vital witnesses to God's kingdom. To

---

1. Dr. Peter L. Steinke argues for a systems approach to understanding congregations using health as a metaphor. He outlines factors that put congregations at risk and factors that promote health in congregations. See *Healthy Congregations: A Systems Approach* (Bethesda, Md.: Alban Institute, 2006). Dr. Steinke says that "like healthy people, congregations promote their health through 'responsible and enlightened behavior.' The people who are most in position to enhance the health of a congregation are precisely those who have been empowered to be responsible, namely the leaders" (xi).

select Teaching Congregations, SFTS considers the full spectrum of congregational development including:

* new church developments (NCDs);
* congregational redevelopments or transformation congregations;[2]
* long-established congregations with enduring vitality.[3]

The designation of a vital and healthy mission-shaped community for internships reflects the SFTS commitment to mentoring in the arts and skills of ministry.[4]

## *Mission-Shaped Communities*

The formation of the first New Testament churches was in response to God's self disclosure, which Karl Hartenstein described in the phrase he coined, *missio Dei.*[5] God sent the prophets of the Old

2. "Redevelopment" congregations may be defined in a variety of ways. For the purpose of this chapter, they are congregations in which the active membership of the church no longer resembles the people in the community where the church building is located (e.g.: there are differences of ethnicity, language, class, or culture between those who are members/regular attendees of the church and those persons who live and work in the community where the church building is located). The PC (USA) has changed the typology of these factors from "redevelopment" to "transformation" congregations — which is the designation used hereafter in this chapter. New Church Developments (NCDs) are new church plants that are brand new congregations.

3. This chapter deals specifically with the Teaching Congregations Initiative, which is defined by and through congregational ministry. However, ministry may take many other forms; therefore SFTS internship requirements may also be met through additional forms of ministry, such as chaplaincies, Clinical Pastoral Education, church-based community organizations, and other approved supervised ministry contexts.

4. The SFTS M.Div. degree expects a successful graduate to be able to serve as an effective church leader. SFTS defines effectiveness through the following learning outcomes: "lead and order services of Christian worship; reflect theologically on Christian faith, the church and the world; provide pastoral care and spiritual formation for individuals and communities; equip churches and communities for mission and ministry." Internships play an integrative role with these learning outcomes. Learning Service Agreements between the intern and mission-shaped congregation supervisor detail the measurable ways the intern discovers, learns, practices, and receives mentoring in "habits and skills" for effective ministry (see footnote 13 on page 73 for a list of "habits and skills").

5. Literally from the Latin, *missio*=sent and *Dei*=God, or "God sent"; that is, the Trinity calls forth and sends the church into the world. The expression *missio*

and New Testament. In the "fullness of time" God sent God's Son, Jesus the Messiah, or Christ. Christ sent the Twelve and the Seventy. At Pentecost, the Holy Spirit empowered the church or "called-out ones"[6] into all the cultures of the world to be witnesses.[7] The Holy Spirit empowered the witness of the church in the world and sealed the presence of the indwelling Christ in those who affirmed faith, became new disciples, and were welcomed into the church.[8] Thus, the prophetic understanding of *mission* arose from, and is modeled by, the activity of the triune God. This Trinitarian understanding reflects the conviction that God has communicated with humanity throughout salvation history and has called a particular people known as the church "to be witnesses" in God's world.

Jesus was the preeminent example of a missionary sent from God — God's own self-disclosure — as is evident in the following

---

*Dei* (the mission of God) is a recent (twentieth century) theological construct that has roots in the patristic era. Western medieval theology articulated the interrelating actions within the Trinity in salvation history as the basis for God's work or mission in the world (see *Dictionary of the Ecumenical Movement,* ed. Nicholas Lossky et al. [Geneva: WCC Publications, 2002], 780–81); Karl Hartenstein coined the term *missio Dei* in 1934 (see "Karl Hartenstein 1894–1952: Missions with a Focus on the 'The End' " in *Mission Legacies: Biographical Studies of Leaders of the Modern Missionary Movement,* ed. Gerald H. Anderson et al. [Maryknoll, N.Y.: Orbis Books, 1998], 591–601). See also David J. Bosch, *Transforming Mission: Paradigm Shifts in Theology of Mission* (Maryknoll, N.Y.: Orbis Books, 1993), 389–93. Bosch documents the use of the term *missio Dei,* which is often attributed to Karl Barth. Building on the Western theological legacy and in particular the Barthian emphasis of *actio Dei* (God's action), Bosch prophetically redefined *mission* from an activity centered in ecclesiology to *mission* defined theologically in the *missio Dei.* That is, *mission* has to do with the very nature of the triune God, who calls and sends the entire people of God (e.g., the church, or body of Christ, not just missionaries) into God's missionary work in the world.

6. The literal meaning of the Greek word for "church" is "called-out ones." This term is borrowed by the New Testament writers from the public square — meaning initially people "called out" for some public meeting purpose — and used in the New Testament as the term for those whom God "calls out" in Christ and then sends into the world on God's mission. The PC (USA) *Book of Order* describes the church as the "provisional demonstration of what God intends for all humanity" (G.3.0200).

7. In Acts 1:8 the meaning of the original Greek text translated "ends of the earth" is a word that could be translated to every "ethnicity" or "culture."

8. Ephesians 1:3–14; see v. 13: "marked with the seal of the promised Holy Spirit."

passage from John's Gospel. Here John equates Jesus as the Word with Jesus as the God who came to earth and lived among us:

In the beginning was the Word, and the Word was with God, and the Word was God. . . . All things came into being through him. . . . And the Word became flesh and lived among us, and we have seen his glory, the glory as of a father's only son, full of grace and truth. (John 1:1, 3a, 14)

Thus, the formation of the church is grounded in a missionary God[9] who sends the "called-out ones" into the entire world in faithful witness of God's reign in Christ.[10]

What does faithful witness to God's reign look like? God's self-witness in Christ's life on earth gives us some clues. Christ demonstrated an advocacy for justice and peace and in doing so he called together a community, those whom he called disciples. As the community follows the One who came "not to be served but to serve and give his life as a ransom for many," there are no credibility gaps or mixed motives. Jesus incarnates the mission involved showing in his words and deeds how to carry out that mission. For example, Jesus was concerned for "the lost" (Luke 15) to be sure — those in need of salvation and grace — but in his ministry we also see consistently his concern for the welfare of the city, for physical health, for just treatment of the oppressed, and for the outcasts of the first century (Luke 10:30–37; Matt. 8:14–17; Mark 10:46–52; Matt. 23:37–39). Thus, the formation of particular mission-shaped communities is an ongoing apostolic pattern for the twenty-first century church. As mission-shaped communities today faithfully embody Christ's call, the church fulfills God's purpose.

---

9. The choice of the term "missionary" in this chapter is informed by the Latin word *missio,* which literally means "sent." Hence, our Triune God is a sending or missionary God. In saying God is a "missionary God," I am making a deliberate attempt to reclaim this term from a missionary movement covering over two millennia that has both positive legacies (faithful Gospel witness) and negative legacies (paternalism, cultural insensitivity, etc.) of extending God's kingdom.

10. The Greek meaning of "apostle" is "sent one."

When the church focuses on Christ's call to make disciples, the church is not reduced to mere private spirituality or inwardly focused expressions of faith. It does not reduce the witness of the church to a glorified United Way by serving others without naming the Name. Faithfully following Christ's call expresses authentic Christocentric witness in contextually vital words and deeds within specific ethnicities and cultures. A mission-shaped community is sent to witness faithfully to God's reign in Christ. This holistic witness involves both fulfilling our Lord's Great Commission of disciple-making and fulfilling Jeremiah's call to God's people in exile to seek "the *shalom* of the city."[11]

Vital witness to God's reign in Jesus Christ is Gospel-centered and contextually engaged. In the first century, faithful communities heard the Good News and translated this news into their ministry contexts. In the time of the early church, this apostolic strategy was held together through common faith in Christ's Lordship and in shared commitment to the continuation of Christ's mission.

Christ's call and formation of disciples (and the subsequent churches formed from that call) has seminal implications for mission-shaped communities in the twenty-first century. The challenge of forming mission-shaped churches today requires a critical review of our theology and practice of ministry. It is in this critical review that we may find a deeper conversion to the Gospel, a Gospel not held captive by any one ethnicity or culture, rooted in the triune God, in order to "make peace through the blood of the cross" (Col. 1:15–20).

The Gospel comes clothed in a culture of the first century, and yet the Gospel transcends the captivity of any single culture by pointing us toward God's kingdom. Mission-shaped congregations embody the hearing of the Gospel for their ministry contexts and, in so doing, re-envision the calling and sending of God's people in ways that respect cultural diversity and challenge social injustice.

---

11. Matthew 28:16–20; Jeremiah 29:7. See also Isaiah's vision of "setting the oppressed free" and a "new earth" in Isaiah 58:5–9.

## Mission-Shaped Teaching Congregations in the SFTS Internship Program

Internships normally occur between the second and third year of theological study and focus on the critical goal of leadership formation. In fact, the mission of SFTS is forming "whole leaders for the whole church." The internship is the centerpiece of integrative studies, for during the internship, classroom learning and theological application are experienced and taught through the church involved in God's world.

The person who mentors interns is central to the internship. It is that person who, in a real sense, bridges the gap between the seminary and the church. Therefore, it is mission-shaped congregations that have established leaders (supervising clergy as well as lay leadership in "shepherding teams") which become the basis for selection.

Established clergy and lay leadership covenant with SFTS to train the current generation of seminarians to be whole leaders for the whole church. Currently, SFTS has more students from diverse racial-ethnic and international backgrounds than any other PC (USA) seminary. Hence, the vision of the "Teaching Congregation" embraces congregations that are culturally, racially, socioeconomically, theologically, and situationally diverse.

These congregations include New Church Developments (NCDs), Transformation Churches, and long-established churches.[12] Placing future church leaders in mission-shaped congregation internships helps assure that these students receive an opportunity to practice and discern ministry habits and skills[13] and to integrate

---

12. Additionally, students could be placed in middle or national governing bodies with a supervisor whose responsibilities engage congregations in mission-shaped strategic planning and programming.

13. The following SFTS list of "Habits and Skills" specify ministry competencies for practice and discernment during an internship:

+ Lead a congregation in Reformed worship.
+ Preach literate, thoughtful, scripture-based sermons.
+ Provide pastoral care and counseling.
+ Educate a congregation in the faith.

their studies with ministry praxis at a critical period of their development.[14]

The supervisor of an intern is viewed as an extension of or adjunct to residential faculty. Supervisors collaborate closely with SFTS through the Northern California and Southern California offices overseeing Field Education and through the student's faculty advisor. Additionally, there is a close collaboration with the student's ordaining body, which for PC (USA) candidates involves their Committee on Preparation for Ministry and subsequent Committees on Ministry.

## An Example of a Mission-Shaped Congregation and Supervision

An example of an SFTS Teaching Congregation is the Calvary Presbyterian Church of San Francisco, where Dr. Laird Stuart is the long-established pastor.[15] The mission statement of Calvary Presbyterian Church states:

Calvary Presbyterian Church is a community of believers:
United by faith, scripture, and the constitution of our denomination
Committed to calling all people to Christ

---

◆ Manage the practical affairs of a congregation.

◆ Articulate the global witness and mission of the church and foster participation in its evangelistic task.

◆ Articulate personal faith and nurture the spiritual life of a congregation and its members.

◆ Lead in ethical witness to society, challenging public evil and cultivating the common good.

◆ Apply theological education in non-congregational ministries.

14. Normally an internship placement starts after the first half of seminary studies has been completed and is finished prior to the senior year of study.
15. Dr. Laird J. Stuart has been pastor and head of staff of Calvary Presbyterian Church in San Francisco since 1993.

And encouraging each other in faith
Through worship, education, fellowship, and service.[16]

This statement, which was approved in 1994, underscores many biblical passages describing God's mission. Dr. Stuart says the text that best describes the mission focus desired is "the ending of Matthew's Gospel, specifically Matthew 28:16–20, frequently called 'The Great Commission.' "

Focusing on the Great Commission, the governing body of Calvary, the church Session, strategized how to organize for this mission. According to Dr. Stuart, the result was five commissions of Session, which focused on this new priority: Worship, Education, Fellowship, Service, and Support. "The Support Commission" was formed to oversee the stewardship of resources that fund the other commissions.

The mission vision was focused in forthcoming years to include core values that honored the vision and suggested steps toward fulfillment. The following value statement was adopted and included as an elaboration of the mission statement:

*To fulfill our mission, we strive to be:*

*Christ-centered*

> To make our faith in Jesus Christ the core of our existence.

> To be accountable to Jesus and to allow Him to influence and guide our life's decisions.

*Spiritually Vital*

> To be awake to God's presence in our lives.

> To work toward a stronger relationship with God.

> To be constantly renewed and refreshed with the power and grace of our living, loving God.

---

16. For a complete listing of education, fellowship, and service opportunities see *www.calvarypresbyterian.org.*

*Evangelistic*

> To exhibit through word and deed a life that benefits from, and freely witnesses to, the belief that Jesus is Lord.

> To share our belief in God with others.

> To encourage others to make personal commitments to Christ.

> ... and to respond to Christ's call for:

*Service to Others*

> To serve God and God's people with our time, talents, and treasures.

> To love and nurture others as God loves and cares for us.

> To put the concerns of others before our own.

> To care for others who may not have the ability to care for themselves.

> To manage our church's resources so we can continue to serve future generations.

*Courage in Faith*

> Boldly to follow Jesus' example in leading our lives.

> To keep our faith despite difficulties.

> To welcome the expression of divergent views while remaining faithful to the community.

> To listen to and follow God's lead in times of uncertainty.

*Justice*

> To respond to others with compassion, not judgment.

> To acknowledge human rights as universal, and to support aspirations for human justice unbiased by social, political, economic and racial distinctions.

> To serve our community without turning away from the needs of others whom we see as unlike ourselves.

Dr. Stuart candidly reflects:

> the degree to which a congregation lives into and honors a mission statement is always subject for reflection and even debate. One of the ways at Calvary that we try to keep this mission statement alive in our collective spirit is by going through periodic evaluations of our life together in Christ.

This conviction launched a review and integration process in continuous five-year planning. This process brought orderly adjustments and creative changes that addressed contextual needs and expectations in coming years.

Dr. Stuart credits the Planning Team resource of *Holy Conversations* by Gil Rendle and Alice Mann for seminal ideas in this process.[17] This resource brought a fresh perspective to their mission planning process. Stuart states:

> It identified "problem planning" as the type of planning which addresses a specific problem and asks "How do we fix it?" It identified "developmental planning" as the process by which a group asks itself the question "what's next?" Then it described 'frame-bending planning' as the effort to take a more radical step in looking forward. In "frame-bending planning" the whole framework of a congregation's life is purposely bent, in the analysis of the people engaged in planning to see if there is a new way God wants us to look at ourselves and our mission. As it is described in the book, "Frame-bending planning, in a similar way, is a process designed to highlight and disturb expectations in order to make space for the possibility of an unseen or unconsidered future."[18]

For Calvary to continue in a missional trajectory of being shaped by God's "frame-bending," the congregation had to be involved with a plan that was introduced in 2005. Dr. Stuart highlights the following aspects of this plan:

---

17. Alice Mann and Gil Rendle, *Holy Conversations* (Bethesda, Md.: Alban Institute, 2003).
18. Ibid., 9.

- Use of Christian practices to help leadership rediscover and be inspired by the presence of God in their activities at church.

- Use of more silence in worship and other events.

- Renewed practices of good stewardship in worship.

- Seeking of ways to make education at Calvary more of a spiritual experience and less intellectual or academic.

- Clarity of contextual focus on providing a more moderate voice for Christian faith in light of the more strident expressions of Christian faith currently evident in society.

Their mission-shaped focus also included the welcoming and training of twenty-first century church leaders, namely seminary interns. Stuart says that he hopes that interns "perceive our devotion to this mission and also become aware of our struggles and foibles as well as our accomplishments and joys in living into this mission."

A Learning Service Agreement[19] between Calvary, the intern, and SFTS engages the intern in multifaceted aspects of congregational life and the internship requirements of theological reflection papers, discipleship practices, preaching, etc. Mentorship or supervision of the intern moves beyond weekly administrative meetings about ministry assignments into theological reflection, feedback, prayer, and ministry skill development. Alongside mentoring supervision, the intern receives congregational lay leader feedback and prayer support through a congregational Shepherding Committee. They reflect with the intern on the firsthand experiences of internship ministry from a lay purview.[20]

San Francisco Theological Seminary has identified four learning outcomes it wants its students to acquire during the course of their education. They are:

1. Lead and order services of Christian worship.

2. Reflect theologically on Christian faith, the church, and the world.

---

19. For a Leaning Service Agreement template see the *www.sfts.edu.*
20. For the description and role of a Shepherding Committee see the *www.sfts.edu.*

3. Provide pastoral care and spiritual formation for individuals and communities.

4. Equip churches and communities for mission and ministry.

Internships play an integrative and central role in these learning outcomes.

A Teaching Congregation such as Calvary is the heartbeat of praxis linking the academic dimensions of theological education and contextualization, where the intern encounters in a congregation what a mission-shaped church looks, talks, and acts like. Dr. Stuart articulates his purposes in contextualization as follows:

> It is important for supervision to help the seminary intern practice a faithful stewardship of his or her hope for the church and ministry. Congregational life can often be discouraging and disheartening. It is important to honor those occasions and yet to help the seminary intern not to be spiritually disheartened. It is important for supervision to help the seminary intern see and acknowledge his or her gifts and competencies for ministry. Doing ministry teaches us a great deal about what we can do and what we are not suited to do. Being an intern can be a wonderful opportunity to explore such discoveries. It is likewise important for supervision to help a seminary intern learn how to honor the craft of ministry. By "craft of ministry" is meant both the skills of ministry and the spirit with which those skills are deployed and animated. It is important for supervision to help the seminary intern learn how to appreciate the context for his or her ministry: the social context, the theological context, the heritage of the context and the shared hopes or fears of it. Finally, in this brief review of purposes for evaluation, it is obviously crucial to help the seminary intern reflect upon and discern with more honesty and integrity his or her own call to ministry. Intern ministry can be a time to explore both the validity of a call and the direction to which it is pointing.

## *Intern Reflection*

In order to present a glimpse of internship ministry in a mission-shaped congregation we turn now to a brief theological reflection by an SFTS intern at Calvary Presbyterian Church. Beverly Brewster was an M.Div. student at SFTS and intern at Calvary Presbyterian Church during 2007. She is a second career student who previously practiced law in New York and San Francisco.[21] The following are some of the verses of Scripture that have been formative for her practice of ministry with Calvary.

> Immediately aware that power had gone forth from him, Jesus turned about in the crowd and said, "Who touched my clothes?" ... [T]he woman, knowing what had happened to her ... told him the whole truth. He said to her, "Daughter, your faith has made you well; go in peace, and be healed."
>
> (Mark 5:30–34)

> Very truly I tell you, the one who believes in me will also do the works that I do.                                     (John 14:12)

> ... in Christ God was reconciling the world to himself ... and entrusting the message of reconciliation to us.   (2 Cor. 5:19)

Brewster comments:

> Jesus' teachings about power and relationship and Paul's teaching about the mission of reconciliation were hard to grasp then, and they are still widely misunderstood. To effectively educate a congregation in the faith, one must be prepared to bring to the surface prevailing presumptions about power, relationship dynamics, and mission, and engage participants in a dialogue of mutual growth in understanding.

Brewster believes that faith in Christ is meant to be "empowering, healing, inclusive, and active, and that the education *process* should

---

21. For further background about Beverly Brewster and for the listing of other Calvary Presbyterian Church staff, see *www.calvarypresbyterian.org*.

be all of those, mirroring the content." In her internship at Calvary she and her supervisor, Dr. Stuart, agreed to a Learning Service Agreement that detailed in measurable and accountable ways the internship ministry engagements and practices. The agreement was like a road map that outlined responsibilities for ministry, such as crafting and implementing of educational programs. These responsibilities were consistent with the mission focus of Calvary, which is "holistic, interactive, empowering, and integrated, bringing education, worship, fellowship, and service together, for a Spirit-filled experience."

Brewster expresses gratitude for her supervisor, Dr. Stuart, who saw in her leadership skills and, therefore, "entrusted [her] with Calvary's Social Witness Mission Team, which had a stated purpose of educating the congregation about issues of social justice in the world so as to encourage service." Just prior to Brewster's leadership on this ministry team it had stalled because of "differences in priorities and passions." She listened and learned through several meetings and through email. She reports that she "was able to move the team from unproductive debate into consensus so as to move them forward into action, resuming their ministry to the congregation." This led to scheduling three "Katrina Nights" for the Sundays concurrent with the two-year anniversary of Hurricane Katrina's landfall. She began making preparations with the team for an educational series "along the lines (ministry focus) described above." The story is best told in her own words:

> In the planning and implementation of the "Katrina Nights" program, the team and I stayed mindful of our call to be faithful witnesses to God's reign, remembering Christ's advocacy for justice and peace, the importance of community, the Great Commission, and God's concern for the least of those among our world community. The planning of the educational events was an inclusive, collaborative, and empowering experience. The Adult and Youth Mission Teams joined forces with Social Witness and all thereby gained energy and enthusiasm. Two filmmakers were brought in, one an esteemed academic whose

film was premiering on PBS, the other, a young and talented daughter of a member needing encouragement and a sense of belonging.

A Spirit-filled enterprise attracts volunteers, and indeed, a member felt moved by the Spirit to offer to cook a Cajun dinner open to the entire congregation and any passers-by who might wish to join us to encourage attendance at our educational program. We sent out invitation postcards to Calvary's entire mailing list, and I preached a sermon entitled "People, Pets and Pictures," with the message that God's priorities resemble flood priorities. I took that opportunity to talk up the program and its theological and scriptural framework from the pulpit. The publicity itself served our educational purpose. It called attention to the revitalized teams and their missions and ministries, and it reminded all recipients that the justice issues made evident in the aftermath of Katrina were still alive and unresolved. Unfortunately, many lives were changed forever by Katrina, and many are still suffering.

When the first of the evenings arrived, hospitality and prayer led us into a receptive openness to the witness of film and first-person accounts of the devastation of Katrina and the injustice of the governmental response to the catastrophe. Members of the congregation were visibly moved and shaken, feeling that they cared, as God cares, for those who have been most invisible and marginalized in our society. Through discussion and prayer we supported each other and expressed our solidarity with those from the Gulf region. This is living faith, as Calvin envisioned it, a movement of the heart, not confined to the intellect.[22]

---

22. Calvin says it this way: "we are called to a knowledge of God: not that knowledge which, content with empty speculation, merely flits in the brain, but that which will be sound and fruitful if we duly perceive it, and if it takes root in the heart . . . [Ps. 145: 5–6; Ps. 40: 5] it is also fitting, therefore for us to pursue this particular search for God, which may so hold our mental powers suspended in wonderment as at the same time to stir us deeply" (Jean Calvin, *Calvin: Institutes of the Christian Religion,* vol. 1, ed. John T. McNeill, trans. Ford Lewis Battles [Louisville: Westminster John Knox Press, 2008,] 61–62).

By the final night, our group had tripled in size. We had a great cross-section of the congregation in terms of age and other demographics, as well as some visitors who were brand new to the church. The Cajun dinner was remarkable; just as with the loaves and fishes, the Lord did provide, and we had exactly the right amount of jambalaya for the crowd. Then we screened the slideshow created by our member's daughter, a brilliant compendium of photos and quotes from Calvary mission trips to the Gulf region. What a community building experience; what an education in why we are called to mission!

Finally we screened filmmaker Kate Browne's *Still Waiting, Life after Katrina.* The congregation was raptly attentive, worshipful, throughout. Afterwards, the filmmaker answered questions, and discussion ensued, as we all taught each other what lessons God has for us in studying this disaster and its aftermath. Many questions were asked, especially, What can we do? What more can we do? If we aren't able to participate in mission trips, what can we do?

At this "teachable moment," Brewster says, the "Spirit moved me to share the teachings of the Gospels, articulating my personal faith. Jesus wants us, all of us, to see, and for everyone to be seen" (John 9). She worked with the Calvary team to "share in Christ's establishment of his just, peaceable, and loving world by letting no one be invisible, overlooked, or forgotten."[23] This internship ministry was a process of intentional listening to those who suffer, engaging the ministry context and her leadership in prayer for what they heard, and identifying with those Jesus called the "least of these." Her supervisor, Dr. Stuart, entrusted her with a Calvary team of lay leaders, encouraged her leadership to step out in faith with a stalled witness Team. Her story involves more than hard work and the Spirit-given surprises of educational steps toward faithful discipleship. She comments on the ministry that "there is

---

23. See G-3.0300 in the *Book of Order: The Constitution of the Presbyterian Church (USA)*, Part II 2007/2009 (New York: Office of the General Assembly, Presbyterian Church [USA]).

great value in enlarging our sense of community and shared mission, in truth-telling, and in persistence through prayer. We closed the evening with prayer. This was education that transformed, education that helped us grow. Thanks be to God!"

Indeed, thanks be to God for mission-shaped congregations, supervisors who mentor interns, and most of all the work of God's Spirit through incarnational witness.

# – 7 –

# Contextualizing the Curriculum
## The Communal and Integrative Practices of Theological Education

DAVID O. JENKINS AND P. ALICE ROGERS

Candler School of Theology

THE CONTRIBUTIONS CANDLER HAS MADE to the field of contextual education can be seen in the ways contextual education has become integrated in our curriculum, and also in the ways contextual education has transformed the curriculum. From the beginning of our Supervised Ministry program, which began in 1969, each member of the faculty rotated through small weekly reflection groups designed and co-taught by professors and the site supervisors. This faculty participation and buy-in were essential to the movement toward contextualizing the curriculum, a goal that began taking shape in 1998 with the reformation of Supervised Ministry into Contextual Education. From 1969 to 1998 a culture of theological education at Candler was formed that paved the way for this significant curricular revision.

The inspiration for that revision emerged from the desire of the faculty to contextualize the curriculum rather than isolate contextual education as a separate, albeit required, component of the master of divinity course of study. For thirty years, because of full faculty participation in Supervised Ministry, Candler ethicists conversed with students working at homeless shelters, biblical scholars collaborated with supervisors at a women's prison,

85

church historians listened to students' verbatims of encounters with patients in local hospitals, sociologists informed — and were informed by — a dozen students in a dozen different parishes, systematic theologians engaged in dialog about immigrant and refugee communities, and preaching professors considered their discipline through the lens of adults with developmental disabilities. Students overheard and were invited into conversations going back and forth from ethics to homeless shelters to church to City Hall, from prisons to St. Paul's epistles, from sociology to small, aging parishes, and so on.

In this model, faculty brought their academic interests to bear on conversations emerging from students' experiences of ministry at their sites. Year after year faculty conversed with other cultures, narratives, sets of religious beliefs and practices, in addition to their colleagues and guilds. Their expertise informed and was informed by a myriad of conversation partners, most often the students and supervisors engaged in ministry at these ecclesial, clinical, and social service sites. Students' site experiences redirected a lecture or refined a theological claim. It has been messy, inspiring, uncomfortable, challenging, exciting, and awkward work. Sometimes we have failed to do it well, yet most of the time, creative insights and experiences have been realized.

It also has been complicated work given there are many contexts that require, if not compete for, attention. The multiplicity of contexts include the classroom itself, which is located within the broader contexts of the *academy and the church;* the particular *site* where the student is in ministry, such as a local church, homeless shelter, hospice, or college chaplaincy program; the *local culture* (it matters whether these experiences happen in the Bible-Belt South or the Northwest, whether they occur in a working class, Hispanic, Pentecostal, urban community, or an affluent African American suburban congregation); and the *dominant culture and society* of the United States with its formative values (individualism, materialism, etc.). Even the *historic milieu* functions as context (Is the global economy in crisis such that people are losing their jobs and afraid of the future? Is the world at war? Does it matter that it is post 9/11?). Then there are the *contexts of the students* themselves. Each seminarian has a story shaped by family, neighborhoods, churches, friendships, life's experiences — each formative and each with a voice that still speaks to the conversations at hand. These contexts are simultaneously audiences and constituencies for contextual theological education. By the time students graduate from our seminaries, we hope they will have something theologically worthy and relevant to say to the academy, church, local culture, dominant culture, history, and all the voices from their past.

In addition to having something worthy and relevant to say, we also want students prepared to *act* in those various contexts, believing that contextual education ought to transform ministerial practices as well as theological reflection. Contextualizing the curriculum is the strategy Candler School of Theology has implemented in this sacred task of theological education, a way of communal teaching and learning that engages body and mind. We believe that theological reflection is enhanced when the practices of ministry and knowledge (theological education, practical wisdom) continue to inform and critique the other, and do so in communal settings such as the church and/or small praxis-reflection seminars. Our teaching is held accountable to and by the practical wisdom gleaned from ministry (embodied action) on site, while our actual practices of ministry are held accountable to and by the classroom teaching and critical reflections of the peer group. These convictions, along with thirty years of conversation and experience, have led to the following Integrative Model for contextual education at Candler.

## *Contextual Education I:*
## *Social Service and Clinical Settings*

First-year master of divinity students enroll in one of twelve Contextual Education I sites. These first-year sites include clinical settings (hospitals, hospices) and social service sites (a women's prison, homeless shelters, a day center for adults with developmental disabilities and mental illness, an affordable apartment complex for elderly adults, etc.). There are usually twelve students per site, and they are required to work at that site four hours each week during the academic year. Students generally engage in one-on-one pastoral care ministries with clients and patients, while sometimes also responsible for planning activities, leading worship, managing client portfolios, organizing food or clothing pantries, teaching computer skills to unemployed adults, or simply being with children in after-school programs.

The twelve students at each site are supervised by an agency or hospital employee, usually a chaplain, who has advanced theological education and has been approved by the Candler director of Contextual Education I. Each week in the fall, that site supervisor leads a one-hour reflection group on campus with his or her Candler students. Those conversations focus on the site work and require only a minimum amount of reading and written work.

The twelve students at that site are also enrolled in one of Candler's contextualized Introductory Arts of Ministry (IAM) classes taught by a member of the faculty. In addition to the students at that site, students from one other site are also enrolled in the same IAM class. The IAM courses are introductory "applied" courses, such as Introduction to Preaching, Pastoral Care and Counseling, Urban Ministry, Religious Education, Church and Community Leadership. The professor for that course has worked with the two site supervisors to contextualize the course. For example: twelve Contextual Education I students at Metro State Women's Prison and twelve students at Emory Hospital meet separately each week for one hour with their respective site supervisors, and then these twenty-four students meet together each week for their shared, contextualized Introduction to Pastoral Care and Counseling class. Students at the Decatur Cooperative Ministry (homeless shelters, food and clothing pantries, etc.) and the Emmaus House Poverty Rights Center might be enrolled in Introduction to Urban Ministries. The majority of site-related reading and written work (i.e., case studies, verbatims, journal entries, critical reflection papers) is lodged in this three-hour

IAM class. The supervisors attend that IAM class and sometimes share leadership of the class with the professor.

In this model, the site sometimes functions as a laboratory for the classroom. Skills for ministry are developed, examined, practiced, critiqued, and shaped in dynamic dialectic with classroom lectures, discussions, written assignments, and reflections. In this way students do not feel unprepared or even resentful of the required work on site. They are being equipped throughout their fall semester for the site work. This dialectic also expands the traditional ways of conceiving of and teaching the practices of ministry in the Introductory Arts of Ministry courses, given that the context isn't the local church but might be a prison, hospital, residential center for abused and foster children, or shelter for homeless women and children.

When Introduction to Pastoral Care and Counseling is contextualized — designed for students working each week with hospitalized patients, incarcerated women, or wounded vets recovering from addictions — the course is enhanced by this creative dynamic. Students are unable to keep the course material lodged in a theoretical place in their learning process, but must integrate this learning into their ministerial practices, into their developing theology, and into their maturing identity as pastors. When Introduction to Preaching isn't designed with a local congregation in mind, but rather with adults who are mentally ill and developmentally disabled, we discover that everyone is challenged to rethink what we mean by "proclamation" and how that proclamation is heard as Good News by different "congregations" of disabled, incarcerated, or homeless persons.

For students enrolled in the IAM Introduction to Urban Ministry, as another example, we have also discovered that tried-and-true strategies for community organizing, mapping neighborhood assets, and economic development might need rethinking when students return from their contextual education sites challenging what was taught in the classroom. When those methods did not work in the neighborhood where the students' contextual education is located or in this new economic and political era, how will the professor revise the class? Introduction to Urban Ministry becomes a dynamic, integrative experience for the students, and also for the professors and the site supervisors on staff at the homeless shelters and the job training center as they rethink methodologies — as well as standard texts and academic assignments — in light of this new generation of students and their weekly experiences in particular Contextual Education sites.

Simultaneously, these first-year students are enrolled in Old Testament, History of Christian Thought, and other theology courses in which they encounter a new vocabulary — *theodicy, redemption, justice, atonement, ecclesiology, grace* — which will be informed or challenged by their weekly experiences in Contextual Education.

In the spring term, first-year students meet weekly in a two-hour reflection group co-taught by another faculty member with the individual site supervisor. For instance, a Candler biblical scholar might be partnered with a site supervisor and students from a homeless shelter. The professor would draw from his or her research in Scripture — biblical mandates to care for the poor, Paul's establishment of the Jerusalem fund, scriptural notions of justice, stewardship, or the Jubilee year — and build that into the course syllabus. The site supervisor from the homeless shelter might want students to read articles on domestic violence, welfare policy, mental illness, institutional racism, unemployment, and so on. One can see how attention to the particular site, ranging from hospitals to homeless shelters, as well as the freedom of the professors to draw from their expertise, creates new insights and new syllabi each spring semester. A sociologist of religion will have different concerns and contributions to a discussion of homelessness (or health care, aging, disabilities, incarceration) than an ethicist, systematic theologian, religious educator, American church historian, or homiletics professor.

Because most of our site supervisors stay with our Contextual Education program for many years, they are strengthened by this annual collaboration with new faculty. Likewise, our faculty's interests and practical wisdom are expanded through a change of contextual education settings.

Students are reminded that there is not a template for these fall IAM classes, nor a common syllabus for the spring semester reflection seminars. While we provide guidelines governing the amount of required reading and written work so that students have similar expectations and requirements across the sites and reflection seminars, each class will be different, reflecting the distinctions in sites and unique interests of the faculty.

Since Candler has twelve contextual education sites for first-year students, twelve faculty rotate through the spring semester reflection groups, collaborating with site supervisors on those classes. Each fall another six faculty teach the contextualized Introductory Arts of Ministry groups for those twelve groups. Thus, eighteen faculty each year are engaged in Contextual Education I with first-year students. As we will see, another twelve faculty teach contextualized electives for second-year students in the Contextual Education II ecclesial sites, for a total of thirty faculty who teach contextualized courses each year.

## Contextual Education II: The Ecclesial Year

As with the first year of Contextual Education, the second year involves three components: site work, reflection groups, and integrative course work.

At the end of their first year, Candler students contract with an ecclesial site in which they will engage in the practice of ministry for a minimum of eight hours a week in the fall and spring semesters of their second year. These ecclesial settings include local congregations, campus ministries, and other ministry settings located in a worshiping community of faith. As students identify the ecclesial sites where they will serve, they are encouraged to seek a setting that will broaden and expand their experience of ministry. For instance, students who come from large membership churches are encouraged to engage ministry in a small membership church; if they grew up in a rural area, an urban church; if they have extensive experience in ministerial leadership, they are encouraged to experience ministry in a cross-racial or multicultural setting. Each student's prior formation is unique, and each is encouraged to use the second-year ecclesial setting to expand his or her preparation for ministry.

At each ecclesial site, students are supervised by an ordained minister who has advanced theological education and has been approved by the Candler director of Contextual Education II. This ordained minister agrees to serve as the student's site mentor, providing opportunities for the student to observe and participate in five areas of ministry: preaching and worship, religious education, pastoral and congregational care, outreach and mission, and administration. The site mentor works with the student on issues of vocational discernment, the practice of ministry, and congregational leadership. At the end of each semester, the site mentor prepares an evaluation of his or her Contextual Education student based on observations of the student's weekly work.

While students work on site eight hours per week, they also participate in a three-hour biweekly theological reflection group. Each of these groups has ten students from ten different ecclesial sites in the same geographical region, and each group meets in one of those different settings each time it gathers. The ecclesial sites vary in size, racial and ethnic identity, denomination, theology, liturgy, etc. This arrangement enables students to experience a diversity of congregational contexts and ministerial styles of leadership. They are able to witness how various congregations engage a similar geographical context. Not only do they *hear* reports, verbatims, and case studies from one another's contexts, they actually *see* the physical locations and participate in conversations with one another's site mentors and laity.

Each of these reflection groups is facilitated by an ordained minister who actively serves a local congregation. These teaching supervisors are leaders in their own denomination and are committed to the formation of students engaged in theological education.

The teaching supervisors follow a common framework for readings and assignments; however, they have the freedom to tailor the readings and assignments to the congregations and students represented in their reflection groups. This framework focuses on congregational and community analysis in the fall semester and the practices of ministry as represented in the five areas of ministry in the spring. The readings and assignments are designed to facilitate the students' critical reflections on their congregation and on the larger context in which their site is located. The numerous contexts mentioned in the opening paragraphs of this chapter continue to be in conversation with each other through these diverse reflection groups.

As Contextual Education II students engage in the practice of ministry and communal theological and contextual reflection, they also enroll in at least one of a variety of courses designed by Candler faculty called Contextual Education Electives. These courses are created and designed by each faculty member out of his or her particular discipline and intentionally integrate the work students experience in their ecclesial settings with the learning represented in each particular course. For instance, a professor of Old Testament has designed a course entitled "The Ten Commandments," in which students "focus on an iconic biblical text and the ways in which it has and can be understood in various contexts. These contexts include that of ancient Israel, the history of Christianity, the student's own religious tradition, the student's contextual education site, and popular culture — with special attention to the cinematic interpretations of Krzysztof Kieslowski."[1] The goals of this particular course are: (1) to help students develop their abilities as biblical interpreters, (2) to help students develop their competencies as discussion leaders, (3) to illume the ways in which diverse contexts influence interpretation of biblical literature. Since each student enrolled in this class is working in a Contextual Education II placement, one requirement of the course is to broach the Ten Commandments in that setting. Some examples of possible

---

1. From David L. Petersen's syllabus for OT698, "The Ten Commandments," Fall 2008.

projects include preaching a sermon on the commandment regarding the Sabbath, leading an adult education class focusing on the role of the Ten Commandments in that denomination's traditions, discussing with the building committee the issue of whether the Ten Commandments should be displayed prominently in the church building, viewing De Mille's *Ten Commandments* with a youth group followed by a discussion of the film.

This course on the Ten Commandments is one example of the myriad of courses designed and taught by Candler faculty. These elective groups are intentionally small in number, limited to fifteen Contextual Education II students. Each year eight to twelve of these courses are offered, so that every faculty member creates and teaches a contextual education elective at least once every three years. These courses epitomize the dynamic relationship between the church and the academy as students bring the questions and experiences of the ecclesial settings to the classroom and, in turn, test, observe, and integrate classroom learnings in their particular contexts.

## *Conclusion*

This model of contextual education has enabled Candler to move closer toward its goal of contextualizing the curriculum. It allows students to integrate theological reflection with practices of ministry in classes across the curriculum as the dynamic relationship between context and academy is nurtured. It continues the Candler tradition of full faculty participation in contextual education and ensures that rich conversations continue among ethicists, students working in homeless shelters, biblical scholars, hospital chaplains, church historians, etc.

This model also promotes the fundamental value that praxis-reflection works best in community. Through the reflection groups in both years of Candler's Contextual Education program, these communities of scholars and pastors-in-formation do the complicated communal work of integrating academic material with site ministry. It is an ecclesial practice, as Luke Timothy Johnson suggests, not work to be tackled by isolated individuals. Every task and aspect of the contextual education experience ought to be done as a communal project. Without a community, we are too easily self-deceived about who we are, what is really going on at our site, how we are making pastoral, systemic, and authentic contributions. Faculty, students, and site supervisors are drawn into these communities, which learn from one another, week in and week out. We believe that all of these participants are enhanced by this formative, communal task.

This model of Contextual Education, which has transformed our curriculum and which continues to create dynamic, formative learning communities, is central to the ongoing realization of Candler's mission "to educate — through scholarship, teaching, and service — faithful and creative leaders for the church's ministries in the world."

# PART TWO

# Best Practices of Supervision and Reflection

# - 8 -

# Mentoring for Leadership

## LYNN RHODES

### Pacific School of Religion

S ITE MENTORS ARE FUNDAMENTAL to the formation of seminarians for ministry. The selection and preparation of mentors are vital tasks of theological field educators, and, with faculty and field education directors, mentors share the sacred role of preparing students for leadership in the church and world. For the purposes of this chapter, a mentor is defined as an experienced practitioner who observes and regularly reflects with a seminarian on the work of ministry.

At Pacific School of Religion, we began referring to persons in these roles as "mentors," rather than "supervisors," to better clarify the responsibilities of the role and our expectations of them. Because mentors engage seminarians in vocational discernment and theological reflection, the focus of mentoring is on the seminarian's reflection, not on the supervision of work. When a seminarian spends an hour a week with a competent on-site mentor, the seminarian has the rare opportunity to question and reflect under the guidance and deep listening of one who has observed the seminarian on site and who has the skills to enhance the student's critical self-reflection and growing self-awareness.

Because of the significant role of mentors, our work as field education faculty has become more focused on the formation of mentors and the mentoring relationship with our students. Our specific program asks mentors to attend six mentor education sessions during the academic year. Because the meetings are spaced through-out the year, we are able to develop a deeper discussion among the mentors themselves and to provide support and information as issues arise.

As field educators, we are involved in research and assessment of the issues that face mentors in hopes that our material will be fresh and relevant. As a result of the annual mentor evalua-tions, we discovered that they become committed to the mentoring process when they experience it as invigorating to their own min-istries and learning. Likewise, congregations and agencies become committed to being mentoring communities when they experience themselves as vital to the formation of leadership for their com-munities and denominations, and when they find new possibilities of ministry through the reflection sessions with the seminarians. Often our seminarians are a source of energy and new ideas that give congregations, agencies, and mentors new energy and new challenges.

Even though we have done our own research into the skills of mentoring and believe we offer compelling training and resources, we continue to meet with mentors who know more about the work and issues of ministry than our staff. Therefore, the six annual mentor training sessions always include insights and reflections by mentors on the issues they raise. We try to construct a balance between providing new resources for their work and engaging in collegial discussions that inform all participants.

The mentor training engages or re-ignites the mentors' passion about the work. Theological reflection upon the meaning of the work also leads to excitement about mentoring. Mentor training is effective when the mentor training sessions themselves model theological reflection upon the work of ministry.

Although we address their work as mentors, we begin by focusing on the mentors' hopes for their own ministries and their passion for the work. We ask the question, "What is the meaning of the work?" as often as we ask about the development of competencies for specific work.

## Focus on Learning

One skill of mentoring is helping seminarians examine and articulate what the seminarians need to learn. This is much more difficult than most mentors anticipate it will be, because it is difficult for seminarians, as well as mentors, to focus on learning, not achieving. Seminarians are more open to learning when they start with self-defined learning objectives. When they are accountable for what they want to learn, a major hurdle in mentoring is overcome. In most cases, resistance to learning is decreased and excitement about growth is enhanced.

We start with adult learning theories grounded in the assumption that the seminarian knows herself or himself best. We consider varying learning theories, those that focus on what is most difficult to learn, as well as those that call mentors to deepen the strengths the seminarian brings. Our experience suggests that we need to be flexible, because different students flourish with different approaches. Whichever theories and practices are employed, the attention remains on learning.

Consequently, feedback and assessment of students are linked to the students' learning objectives, rather than accomplishments. Seminarians discover how to acquire and receive feedback on their learning and then they develop the skills to evaluate that feedback. The feedback is not the final step of the mentoring and learning process, but rather one important step in a more complex process.

We have already alluded to the conviction that theological reflection is a communal practice, reflected in the work mentors do with congregations and organizations, as well as with the seminarians. Together they create shared, communal practices of learning, reflection, and growth.

## Relational Dynamics

The quality of mentoring depends upon the level of respect established in the relationship between the mentor and the seminarian, founded on respectful and ethical behavior on the part of the mentor. Mentoring relationships do not need to be close personal relationships. Styles can differ. Theological perspectives can differ. Personalities can differ. What is critical is that the seminarian experiences respect from the mentor. The mentor must be ethical and must be willing to be self-reflective and transparent, thereby modeling the learning process for the student.

The mentor also plays a key role in the relationship the seminarian develops with the church or organization. The mentor addresses a myriad of issues, such as authority, boundaries, and confidentiality. When the seminarian understands that the mentor respects the seminarian, then dealing with these issues is usually constructive. We have had mentors and seminarians who were very different from one another, yet they developed good mentoring relationships because respect was established early on. Because the mentor has more power in the relationship, it is the mentor's responsibility to initiate this respect of the seminarian.

The mentor relationship focuses on the learning and self-reflection of the seminarian, not on the needs or issues of the mentor. There are key boundary issues. It is inappropriate for the mentor to use this time to air her or his concerns, personal issues, competencies, and accomplishments. In mentoring, the relational gift of the mentor is the gift of attentive listening and questioning so that the seminarian has ongoing and regular times to reflect upon her or his own theological and vocational development.

The mentor is not the seminarian's counselor. If counseling issues arise, the mentor should refer the seminarian to someone else for that relationship. It is often difficult to distinguish counseling issues from a mentoring issue, but when students' personal issues raise questions about their pastoral abilities and site work, the mentor needs to refer the student to a counselor. The roles of therapist and mentor are distinctive roles, with professional ethical boundaries helping limit and define each role.

In years of taping mentor sessions, we have found that a major temptation for mentors is to do most of the talking. The seminarian asks questions. Mentors often believe they have great answers, and they have been waiting for someone to ask. It is exciting to talk about ministry with someone who is actually interested; however, the goal of mentoring is the development of the seminarians' ability to be self-reflective, to be able to seek out feedback, evaluate it, and act. Given these objectives, the seminarian should do most of the talking.

Therefore, when selecting mentors, we look for people who have low ego needs, an ability to listen carefully, and an appreciation and knowledge of the basic elements of mentoring: professional skills, good boundaries, good relational dynamics, and a genuine interest in individual and community flourishing.

## Engaging the Vocation of the Mentor

The mentor training engages or re-ignites the mentors' passion for the ministry. Theological reflection on the meaning of ministry and leadership also leads to excitement about mentoring. Mentor training is most powerful and effective when the mentor training sessions themselves model theological reflection on the work of ministry. The mentors engage in their own leadership formation issues and theological reflection on the meaning of their ministries. They are fully engaged when they see new possibilities for ministry emerge in their reflection sessions with the seminarian.

Mentoring occurs in a particular context of the ministry site, but that context is located within specific institutional, economic, cultural, social, political, denominational, and congregational settings that shape the mentoring process and value certain skills and gifts for ministry. Therefore, mentor training and weekly mentoring meetings with students include analyses of the context of the ministry site and the larger community. Social analysis is foundational for the mentoring process. One of the questions we often use in this regard is "How do we know what we think we know?"

## Mentoring Leaders for the Future

Leadership formation, central to the work of mentors, highlights the ability to discern, to listen carefully, to analyze, to be visionary and imaginative. Because we cannot assume that traditional skills of ministry will be appropriate to new contexts of an ever-changing church and world, we encourage seminarians to learn how to exercise discernment with regard to theological issues for leadership in evolving contexts.

One of the helpful ways to approach theological reflection on the work of ministry is to ask about the metaphors seminarians use for understanding their role. Critical theological reflection on ministry metaphors can reveal the theological assumptions that focus the priorities and limits of the work. Different assumptions about the meaning of ministry emerge if the seminarian sees herself or himself as the wounded healer, the social justice advocate, the community organizer, or the sacramental priest.

The mentor teaches discernment through keen observation, astute questions, and deep listening. The process for a mentoring session is basic. The seminarian presents an issue of ministry that has emerged. The mentor listens and asks questions for clarification of facts and feelings for first-level interpretation. Then the mentor probes deeper to encourage the seminarian to think about different ways of perceiving what has happened. This is accomplished through social analysis and by asking how the resources of Scripture and theology might illumine the situation. Only then do questions of skill and action surface. When mentors do not begin with their own interpretations, new insights for both the seminarian and the mentor may emerge. Mentors have sometimes reflected that they have been repeating the patterns of their work but have not discerned new possibilities until they have engaged the seminarian in the discernment process.

Certain issues continue to surface in leadership preparation. How does one prepare for a future church, society, and world that are constantly changing? How is one prepared to work creatively with conflict? How does one assess the meaning of role and authority? How does one establish good self-care and appropriate boundary keeping? What does it mean to mentor someone who is more gifted in some areas than the mentor? In the mentor training sessions, we converse about the future of our forms of ministry. What sustains us in this work? What do our churches, institutions, societies, and world need as we witness to our faith? Although there is much material on leadership, there is also much disagreement and confusion. As certain denominations lose membership, the list of desired leadership skills expands. It is important that mentor training sessions engage these issues and that Field Education teachers know the field of leadership development and spiritual formation.

## Postscript on Theological Understanding of Work and Vocation

In mentor training, we focus much of our discussion on what it means to engage the seminarian in discerning the work she or he might do. One of the stumbling blocks to vocational discernment that seems to persist with seminarians and denominations is that of call and ordination. The majority of denominations that relate to our school claims to honor the priesthood of all believers. In reality, however, pastors and denominations continue to ask the question, "Are you called?" The implication is that some are not called to ministry. Furthermore, it is a shorthand way of saying that being called suggests being called to certain kinds of religious work that requires ordination.

If we do not want to make *call* an elitist doctrine that applies to the privileged few who make it to seminary-level education, then we need to start with a different assumption. God calls everyone. There is no special call, because all are called to live faithfully. What is at stake is how we live out the call of God in our time, in our contexts, and with our opportunities, skills, and life situations. Whether one goes to seminary or not, one is called. Whether one is ordained or not, one is called. Because most mentors are the professionals in work that is recognized as religious, it can be difficult to move from the role of professionally training new professionals to being open to nurturing vocational discernment. Likewise, it is difficult for many seminarians who also subscribe to *the theology of call* to focus on discernment rather than on ordination requirements.

Mentoring is shaped by how mentors understand ministry and vocational discernment. At heart, it is not about skill development, as critical as that is. There is much good and necessary work that needs to be done in the church and world. God needs everyone involved in that work from whatever place, and with whatever skill, knowledge, or passion. We do not need to fear lack of meaningful work. What we do need to fear is a concept of ministry that perpetuates the myth of special call to ordained work. I believe that mentor education is critical to the future of ministry, especially when it is shaped by our common passion to find work that is relevant, good, and meaningful for ourselves, our faith communities, and our fragile world.

# – 9 –

# Bridging Classroom and Parish

## *The Role of Supervision*

MARK DIEMER, LANDIS COFFMAN,
RUTH FORTIS, JANE JENKINS

Trinity Lutheran Seminary

O NE OF EIGHT SEMINARIES in the Evangelical Lutheran Church
in America, Trinity Lutheran Seminary, Columbus, Ohio,
places a significant emphasis on contextualizing the preparation and
education of future clergy of the ELCA. This emphasis is inherent in
the three contextual requirements completed by master of divinity
students preparing for ordination in the ELCA. These requirements
include two years of Ministry-in-Context, a full-time internship
completed during the third year of seminary, and a quarter of supervised clinical ministry which is fulfilled most often by participation
in an approved clinical pastoral education program. Each student
also participates in an Integrative Group during each of the three
years of academic study. At the heart of these requirements is the
supervisory relationship students have with clergy chosen to participate in the Contextual Education program. This supervisory
relationship provides an important bridge between the classroom
and parish as supervising pastors provide a model for ministry,
imparting wisdom on the nuts and bolts of daily parish ministry, and
also model intentional theological reflection in the supervisory conversations. In this chapter, we provide an overview of our program
and overhear two of our intern supervisors as one contributes his

perspective on the training workshop for supervisors and another provides an example of a supervisory relationship with an intern.

## *The Program*

During the first two years at Trinity Lutheran, master of divinity students participate in the Ministry-in-Context program. This program is designed to afford students an opportunity to observe and gain experience in pastoral ministry and to promote critical reflection on these observations and experiences prior to their year-long internship.

Congregations and pastoral supervisors in the local area are invited each July to participate in the program. They provide information about the congregation, including the learning opportunities in their particular context, the pastoral leadership style, the mission goals, and the program requirements. That information is compiled and distributed to incoming students during new student orientation along with a written explanation of the program.

After the fall semester begins, a Ministry-in-Context Supervisor Fair brings potential supervisors to campus for informal conversations with students. Based on the written information and the conversations held, students then choose four or five sites to visit on a Sunday morning for worship. Students are encouraged to visit a Ministry-in-Context site that will take them out of their comfort zone and provide them with experiences unlike what they have known before. After this time of visitation, they submit their top three placement requests. Together with the student, the director ascertains which site might provide a challenging contextual learning experience. By mid-November, the assignments are posted and students begin worshiping and establishing relationships in that congregation.

If students have already had extensive parish experience and have preached, taught, visited, served on council, and worked with various groups, we look for another kind of contextual site to expand their horizons for ministry. There are several campus ministries, a hospital chaplaincy, a nursing home chaplaincy, a drug and alcohol center chaplaincy, and various ecumenical congregations that serve as assignments for those already well formed in Lutheran congregations.

In recent years, Trinity Lutheran Seminary has seen an increase in commuting students who are not in the Columbus area for worship on Sundays. In those cases, the students identify congregations within a half-hour commute of their home, different from their home congregation, and ones where they will most likely be challenged in their learning. At that point, the director of the Ministry-in-Context program contacts the clergy in the congregations, explains the program, and enlists his or her participation as a Ministry-in-Context supervisor.

The first-year of Ministry-in-Context, from December to May, is considered the year of observation/reflection. The goal is for students to enter congregations where they have had no previous involvement and to begin to develop their pastoral identity. They worship at the sites regularly and attend meetings, classes, and events six hours a week. They are specifically encouraged to observe those activities of parish ministry where they have little or no prior experience. When they enroll in the Ministry of Worship class, they are asked to help with worship leadership in a number of ways: as lector, writer of prayers, assisting minister, etc. They meet at least monthly with their supervisor to discuss their observations, to ask questions, and to learn about how the pastor plans for pastoral functions that may or may not be covered in the seminary curriculum. The goal is to take the practical learning of the parish into classroom discussions and classroom learning into the parish. Students document their insights in a log, which is read in May by their faculty advisor, who determines whether requirements for Ministry-in-Context have been met. The advisor writes a brief paragraph stating whether first-year requirements have been met and offers suggestions for learning in the second year.

In the second year of Ministry-in-Context, students continue their service in the same congregation while taking ministry classes in education, pastoral care, and homiletics. They are asked to teach several consecutive class sessions with lesson plans, to make a variety of pastoral care visits, and to preach once or twice. They are to be involved in the congregation for about ten hours a week. Again, they are expected to keep an ongoing reflective log in which they outline significant learnings and other pertinent reflections about their developing pastoral identity. That log is read by the faculty advisor, who writes a paragraph indicating successful completion of the Ministry-in-Context requirement, observations about areas of ministry the student may wish to concentrate on while in internship, and strengths and weaknesses for ministry.

At some point in the second year, each student writes a critical incident to be shared in their small Integrative Group. The review of these incidents in a small group affords students the opportunity for peer evaluation, models the action/reflection practice valued at Trinity, and begins to prepare students for writing verbatims in Clinical Pastoral Education and critical incident reports during their internship year.

Twice during each academic year, Ministry-in-Context supervisors are invited to spend a morning on campus. They share ideas and questions about how the year is progressing with their students, and they meet with faculty who teach core courses and make assignments that are completed in the Ministry-in-Context congregations. Sometimes a session is held on a topic pertinent to pastoral development such as devotional life, crisis intervention, or introduction of a new hymnal. In an effort to show our appreciation for partnership in educating future leaders of the church, Ministry-in-Context supervisors are invited to take one course per year per student, either for credit or audit. If they wish, they may offer that course to another paid staff person in their congregation.

During the third year of study at Trinity Lutheran, students participate in a full-time internship, most often in a congregational setting. It is during this year that students are encouraged to pay specific attention to the issues of vocation and call, skill development and enhancement, congregational analysis and pastoral realities, theological reflection, and the integration of their academic experience with the realities of parish ministry. The director of Contextual Education coordinates this year of internship, matching students with internship sites, making a yearly visit to the student, pastor/supervisor, and congregation, while coordinating the supervisor training. When the students return for their senior year, they enroll in the Pastoral Leadership class, which enables them to process and further explore their experiences from the year of internship.

As students enter into the two-year Ministry-in-Context experience and the full-time year of internship, we expect supervisors and mentors to engage their students in conversation about numerous ministry topics. The areas of discussion include, but are not limited to, one's own experiences of God and personal faith story; the church's theological heritage and its intersection with parish ministry; issues concerning administration of the sacraments; pastoral and theological approaches for dealing with illness, tragedy, and trauma; and the congregation's function in public life and community.

Theological reflection is also a heavily accentuated part of the supervisor's relationship with the student. In the supervisor training workshop, concerted effort is made to differentiate between the roles of counseling, spiritual direction, and theological reflection. The supervisor functions solely in a supervisory capacity for the student/intern, overseeing the student in the daily tasks of ministry and focusing on the theological integration of ministry. If the need arises for the student to engage in personal counseling, the supervisor can facilitate identification of a professional in that field. If spiritual direction is desirable for the intern, here too, the supervisor guides the student to the appropriate resources. Theological reflection — relating biblical, theological, and historical disciplines with the realities of daily acts of ministry — is the foundational role of the supervisor. This practice gives a depth and breadth to the year of internship and establishes an ongoing pattern for doing ministry throughout one's life.

## The Practice

In the two sections that follow, Pastor Mark Diemer of Grace of God Lutheran Church in Columbus, Ohio, and Pastor Landis Coffman of Trinity Lutheran Church in Akron, Ohio, contribute perspectives on the supervisor training workshop and an example of a supervisory relationship with an intern. Each has served as an intern supervisor for many years and has helped lead the supervisor training workshop.

### The Supervisory Training Process (Mark Diemer)

The process for internship supervision at Trinity Lutheran Seminary needs to be experienced in person. The participating pastors attend a three-day workshop which offers training for new supervisors. This training models the supervisory relationship expected to develop during the intern year. Therefore, pastors bring two case studies/critical incidents that will be used during the workshop. The case studies/critical incidents are prepared in either a narrative or verbatim format and are approximately one page in length, focusing on a current ministry incident or concern of the pastor.

In a brief introduction to the workshop, new supervisors are led through a review of the internship manual with special attention given to the important aspect of intern supervision called "Supervisory Time." A major portion of the training workshop is used to observe, experience, and lead the theological reflection process that will be experienced in supervision.

The process begins as one pastor presents a case study/critical incident and another engages the experience as a supervisor. Each participant, as well as the workshop trainers, presents and supervises twice. As presentations are made, the remaining workshop participants observe the supervisory session and offer observations and feedback, not on the content of the ministry event being discussed, but on the manner of the supervisor, the theological direction, and ministry examination of the case.

In the course of the three-day workshop, both participants and trainers hone and demonstrate the skills of supervision. Differences in style and approaches to supervision become apparent, and the advantages of these alternatives and techniques offer ways each supervisor can enhance and develop his or her own individual style of supervision.

Conversation during the supervisor training workshop also includes how best to utilize the case study/critical incident model during supervision. Such practices include having the student provide the supervisor with the case study/critical incident at least twenty-four hours in advance so that the supervisor can preview the case and begin prayerful consideration of the issues presented — making sure the supervisory sessions are frequent, consistent, and uninterrupted and seeing that no other matters are discussed until the case study or critical incident and theological reflection supervisory time is concluded.

Throughout the supervisor training there is considerable conversation about the task and relevance of theological reflection in the process of reviewing case studies/critical incidents. Supervisors and interns are encouraged to include these five stages in each session: clarification of the incident, evaluation of the issues, exploration of the issues, theological reflection, and direction for how to move on with this ministry issue. The important task of differentiating theological reflection from counseling and spiritual direction is repeatedly addressed. Also discussed during the training workshop are supervisory and ministry themes that may occur and/or reoccur in internship, the four-pane Johari window,[1] constructive feedback, and ways to help the student cultivate his or her own ministry style.

In the three days of the supervisor training workshop, there is immediate feedback on one's supervisory skills and, in the course of that feedback, modeling of how to offer evaluation and critique. The supervisor training workshop concludes with the pastor/participants evaluating themselves and colleagues as well as the workshop trainers.

---

1. A Johari window is a cognitive psychological tool developed by Joseph Luft and Harry Ingham in 1955. It is used to help people better understand how they are known by self and others, known by others but not self, known by self but not others, and unknown by self or others.

To further encourage theological reflection during the year of internship as we look to the future, a new requirement is being explored and evaluated for possible implementation by the Contextual Education director and committee. Students will be expected to assemble a portfolio of six case studies/critical incidents with accompanying theological reflection completed during the intern's supervisory sessions. These two- or three-page reports — one page for the ministry incident and one or two pages for subsequent theological reflections — would be submitted to the seminary's Contextual Education office, along with the required periodic internship evaluations currently in place. The ministry incident/theological reflection portfolio will assist in evaluating the student's progress during internship and also provide material for senior level classes where the internship year is further processed. If the student chooses, the portfolio material could also be shared with the student's faculty advisor, thereby giving the faculty person a perspective on the student's theological growth as well as further informing the faculty person about current issues in a congregational setting.

### The Practical Application (Landis Coffman)

When I receive an intern, our time together begins with a two-day retreat in which we read *The Way of the Heart* by Henri Nouwen. The content of this book opens our minds to a spiritual and theological basis for our relationship as mentor and intern. As we get to know each other, we discuss and share our expectations, hopes, and dreams for the year.

An intentional part of this retreat is our discussion of the supervisory process. I remind my student to review the internship orientation and the internship manual pages on supervision, and we discuss together the following:

- Supervision is the single most important experience of the intern year.
- It is a weekly event. It is not a "nuts and bolts" discussion. It is not a book review, Bible study, or casual conversation.

- Case studies/critical incidents are discussed during supervision. These papers are to be handed to me twenty-four hours before the supervisory session. This gives me time to digest the incident, analyze the content, and choose a process for the discussion ahead.

- The supervisory session is held in a location that reduces interruptions. Ninety minutes is suggested for the length of the session. More sessions on one topic can emerge from a single case study presentation.

- If persons of the parish are discussed within the written piece, false names should be used to assure confidentiality and anonymity. The completed incidents will be kept by me in a secure location. If identities are still apparent, the papers will be shredded following the sessions.

- As supervisor I may suggest a topic for a session. This topic might center on an issue upon which reflection is needed for the intern's experience and development. In this case, I might write about a critical incident in my own life and the intern might function as the discussion leader.

During the course of the internship, the intern and I are attentive to the task of theological reflection as we discuss case studies/critical incidents in our supervisory sessions. Guiding questions are: Where is God in this? Where are you in this? What would you do as a pastor in this situation? Does the Word of God enter your mind? What does this say to you about your words, your actions, your faith, the church? We also role play certain situations in which the intern functions as the pastor, and I play the parishioner. This enables the intern to identify with pastoral functions and tasks, and I simply help facilitate pastoral identification.

On occasion, an intern will ask, "Can we do away with supervision this week because I am so busy?" and I reply, "Busyness is a reality in a pastor's life. You must learn how to juggle tasks and choose what is really important. Write up your critical incident!"

In the supervisory sessions there will be moments of vocational, theological, and personal insights. But there will also be moments of frustration, disappointment, and aggravation. All of these moments are important and worthy of intentional conversation.

As a supervisor, I have found it important to call upon God to strengthen, heal, direct, and support my leadership. I believe that as an intern supervisor, I should reflect a presence of servanthood and discipleship. I want my interns to depart each session with a sense of "putting on Christ," as St. Paul affirmed. I hope that they can say, "I can see it; therefore, I can do it. I am God's person." I want all of my interns to be able to say this about supervision: "I gained new insights about pastoring from every session."

## *Conclusion*

As seen in the above reflections, the supervisory process helps bridge the gap between the classroom and the parish while supporting Trinity Lutheran's goal to integrate the traditional academic disciplines of biblical studies, theology, and church history with the daily realities of parish ministry. As students participate in the Integrative Groups, the Ministry-in-Context program and the internship year, we hope that the important task of integration enriches and deepens the ministry of each clergy candidate, as well as the church.

# – 10 –

# How Not to Praise Your Intern

## *The Role of Observation in Ministerial Formation*

### BARBARA J. BLODGETT

### Yale Divinity School

I N THE FIFTH CHAPTER of the book of Daniel, we hear the story of the court servant Daniel being summoned by King Belshazzar to decipher and interpret a mysterious writing that has appeared on the wall of the royal palace. Daniel is an exile from Judah who had been brought into the king's court by King Belshazzar's father, King Nebuchadnezzar. His reputation for having great wisdom precedes him. The mysterious inscription on the wall unnerves King Belshazzar because he lacks the ability to read it, let alone understand it. He has heard about Daniel's reputation, and his queen is urging him to solicit Daniel's help, but it wounds his pride to do so.

Perhaps because of his insecurity, or perhaps out of pride, King Belshazzar believes he must offer Daniel three rewards for interpreting the writing. "You shall be clothed in purple," he tells Daniel, "have a chain of gold around your neck, and rank third in the kingdom" (5:16, NRSV). Daniel rejects these tokens, saying: "Let your gifts be for yourself, or give your rewards to someone else! Nevertheless I will read the writing to the king and let him know the interpretation" (5:17). Daniel agrees to offer his skills, but he will do so for his own reasons and on his own terms. He rejects the bribery implied in the gifts of imperial power. The story concludes with Daniel interpreting the writing with ease. It turns out to be a withering indictment of King Belshazzar. That night the king is killed and a new king takes the throne.

It would have been easy for Daniel to give in to the seduction of power and prestige represented by being asked to assist the king. And yet by resisting reward, Daniel claims a measure of freedom from his enslavement by the royal court and its powers and principalities. This moment of individual achievement suggests a metaphor for resisting praise. Praise is one kind of reward that is all too easily bestowed and all too happily received.

There are many kinds of "rewards" we receive in life, often for doing what we would have done anyway, such as Daniel's interpretation. Think of Employee of the Month awards, class rankings, gifts for years of service at our jobs. Praise is one of these rewards. In recent years, I have mounted a small campaign at Yale Divinity School to encourage my supervisors not to praise their interns. I believe that praising people for attributes such as intelligence, natural ability, artistry, and so on, does not necessarily motivate them to do better and may even have negative consequences. While most of us accept the idea that we should not label people for their shortcomings — in theological terms we should hate the sin but not the sinner — many people still seem to insist upon labeling people for their giftedness. But why should this be? Why not "love not the gifted one but the giving itself"? I tell my supervisors *not* to tell their interns "You're the greatest preacher," or "You're a natural born pastor," but rather to talk about the actual act of the preaching or the pastoring instead.

I hasten to clarify the distinction between praise and feedback, as I am using these terms. Praise is simply a blanket statement of how good someone is, without explaining what in particular they are good at and what is good about it. Some call this "empty praise." It is a laudatory comment directed toward persons *qua* persons, that is, toward their attributes or qualities rather than their performance. "You're a math genius." "You're such a gifted singer." "You have a pastor's heart." "You've inherited your daddy's artistic gene."

Feedback, in contrast, is a statement about the nature of what someone did. It is directed not toward a person's attributes but toward their performance. So, for example: "I admire the work you did to get a ninety-eight on that math quiz." "Your singing makes me feel so serene." "I can tell that you brought comfort to that grieving family." "You use the most vivid colors in your paintings." Note that feedback can be just as positive and approving as praise; it just adds more detail and shifts the focus away from a person's identity and to the effort and engagement they put into their task.

I wish to underscore this last point. By differentiating between praise and feedback, I am not differentiating between positive and negative. It is not that praise consists of positive statements and feedback of negative ones, because feedback can be either positive or negative. Apparently, there are some educators who do not believe in positive statements of any kind. A student of mine told me that for the entire summer her Clinical Pastoral Education (CPE) supervisor refused to say anything positive about her work, even when she specifically asked him for positive feedback. Instead, he apparently told her that she needed to develop her own internal sense of positive feelings about her work. Now he may be on to something, but I do not happen to subscribe to his educational philosophy. I have always believed people learn from their successes as well as their failures, so there is value in detailing the positive aspects of what someone has done.

In my one-person campaign to teach supervisors how not to praise their interns, I have come across several forms of resistance. After all, who doesn't like being praised? It feels good, and the idea that we can inspire people to higher levels of learning and achievement by praising them is an idea that dies hard. We tend to think, like King Belshazzar, that praise should naturally accompany our efforts to get people to do what we want them to do. We also think that if someone lacks the necessary confidence to perform better, our praise will supply it. Finally, we assume that without praise our students might not discover their gifts. I am doubtful of all of these claims (that praise inspires, motivates, and teaches). It is not at all clear to me that people would not work just as hard, perform just as highly, and know what they are good at, without our laudatory comments.

I have discovered, looking into the work on praise, that I am not alone in my hunches. Let me offer some of the research and theory illustrating that people work just as hard, perform just as highly, and know what they are good at, without praise. In fact, as it turns out, they often do even better.

Chief among the growing number of educators and scholars who have studied praise is social psychologist Carol Dweck, formerly of Columbia University and now at Stanford University. Dweck believes that success of many kinds — excelling in sports, succeeding in business, doing well in school — is ultimately aided not by boosting people's sense of their natural abilities or attributes, but rather by boosting their engagement in and passion for the task. When it comes to academic achievement, for example, a student is better off believing in their effort than believing in their intelligence.

Dweck's most famous studies involving four hundred students were conducted in fifth-grade classrooms in different regions of the United States. Her researchers gave students a set of nonverbal puzzles that were designed at only a moderate level of difficulty. They all did the puzzles and afterward, they all were told their scores. But, in addition, one group of students were told "You must be smart at this," while another group was told "You must have worked really hard." A third, control group received no additional comment beyond their score. All students were then offered a choice if there were time remaining at the end of the study: (1) to work on problems that were not too hard, so they would not get many wrong, or (2) to work on problems from which they would learn a lot, even if they would not appear so smart. Their choices were revealing: far more children who had been praised for their intelligence chose to work on the easy problems than children who had been praised for their effort. In fact, the data showed that 90 percent of the students who had been told "You must have worked really hard" asked to work on problems from which they would learn.

For the second trial, all students worked on puzzles designed at a seventh-grade difficulty level (two levels above their own). All of them predictably performed less well; this trial was in effect an artificially induced failure. It was designed to see to what students would attribute their failure. When observed and questioned during the test, students in the two groups responded quite differently. Those in the "intelligence" group got visibly distressed and said things like "I guess I wasn't as smart after all" while those in the "effort" group said things like "I guess I'm not working hard enough." These students did not appear discouraged and some even said it was their favorite test. Finally, all the students worked on a third set of problems, this one designed to be as easy as the first. Their scores resulted in a dramatic finding. Across six different versions of the same problem set, those children who had been praised for their effort improved their scores (on average, by 30 percent), while those who had been praised for their intelligence did worse than they had in the very beginning. (Recall that Trial 1 and Trial 3 were the same level of difficulty.) One word of praise actually lowered test scores.[1]

When interviewed later about her study, Carol Dweck said that she and her researchers had a hunch about the detrimental effect of praise, but even they were surprised that one simple comment would make such a difference. Since this study, Dweck has gone on to conduct a great deal more research into praise, on all sorts of people, and she has found that praise has a significant deleterious effect on success. As she explains: "Emphasizing effort gives a child a variable that they can control. They come to see themselves as in control of their success. Emphasizing natural intelligence takes it out of the child's control, and it provides no good recipe for responding to failure."[2]

---

1. Po Bronson, "How *Not* to Talk to Your Kids: The Inverse Power of Praise," *New York Magazine,* February 19, 2007, with additional reporting by Ashley Merryman. See also Claudia S. Mueller and Carol S. Dweck, "Praise for Intelligence Can Undermine Children's Motivation and Performance," *Journal of Personality and Social Psychology* 75, no. 1 (1998): 33–52, and Carol S. Dweck, *Mindset: The New Psychology of Success* (New York: Random House, 2006), chapter 1.

2. Bronson, "How *Not* to Talk to Your Kids," 27.

Dweck believes that what she found in these fifth-graders' experience of being tested is replicated in a pattern dividing all of us. Some of us have what she calls a "fixed mindset" with respect to our capacities. We believe that intelligence, athleticism, musical talent, and other attributes of ours are fixed and given, that we either come into this world possessing them or not, and there is little we can do to change that. Those of us who have such a mindset receive reinforcement in all the messages we receive from an early age telling us we are smart, talented, gifted, and so on. Some of us, on the other hand, believe that our capacity to excel can always be cultivated. Dweck calls this having a "growth mindset." According to the growth mindset, "everyone can change and grow through application and experience," and no one's potential can be known with certainty ahead of time.[3] The growth mindset is detectable in the passion some people have for persisting at their projects and pushing themselves to improve, even and especially when they are not doing particularly well.

A fixed mindset can be detrimental to those who have it because it indisposes them to failure. If I am told my whole life that I am gifted, for quite a while I might do just fine — in part because I will carefully choose activities that guarantee my success and prove my giftedness, just like the fifth-graders. But when the time comes that I fail at something — which is going to happen eventually — I will not be not only disappointed but defeated. I will be ill equipped to cope with my failure. After all, I attribute success and failure to my personhood, my very being. I will be less likely to chalk up my failure to a bad day during which I did not do my best, or to a mistaken strategy, or to prejudice or luck, the way my growth mindset friends will.

Our theological schools are competitive places where students are measuring themselves against each other and against deeply held ideas about who they are and what they are capable of. This includes field education internships. Whether they articulate it or not, many

---

3. Dweck, *Mindset*, 4. The growth mindset pertains, incidentally, even to mindsets, believing not that they are fixed but rather that a person can change from fixed to growth! (*Mindset*, 46).

of our ministry interns are surely asking themselves, "Will ministry come easily to me so that I do well at it?" "Will I be good at this and be a success?" and the close cousin to such questions, "Am I called to this?" (One of my supervisors reported that an intern once asked him directly, "Am I the best intern you've ever had?" a question really more poignant than amusing.) I have had several moments over the years, as many of us probably have, of discovering that a student feels unworthy and doubts her choice of ministerial study. My impulse is to rush in and heap on the praise! But if her supervisor or I respond to her insecurities this way, we may ironically be adding fuel to the fire.

What are some other ways we can respond? We return to the practice of feedback, which I have defined as detailed information tailored to the work an individual has performed.

In order to help wean supervisors from giving praise to providing feedback, I designed an instrument called the Observation Report. Adapted from a technique I learned in the training of student teachers, it requires a supervisor to pay close attention to the student while the student is engaged in practicing some ministry skill. It also invites students to request the specific form of feedback they desire, thus learning how to direct their own learning process. My hope was that the Observation Report would guide supervisor and student in the giving and receiving of concrete and specific assessment. My theory was that some supervisors praise their interns because they do not have or take the time to offer feedback. A universal blanket statement such as, "You're so great," makes up for that insufficiency.[4]

The Observation Report is completed in three parts. First, the interns write down what skill they are working on in the activity being observed, what their personal and professional goals are, what they want their supervisor to watch for, and what they are hoping to contribute to their site through this ministry. Then the supervisor watches the intern doing ministry. Finally, the supervisor

---

4. Bronson, "How *Not* to Talk to Your Kids," 83.

addresses the intern's questions and adds any additional feedback that is especially pertinent but for which the intern may not have asked. The first-year I assigned Observation Reports, in 2006–7, was trial.[5] The results prompted several reflections on the challenge of getting supervisors not to praise their interns.

First, I noticed a tendency that I call "collusion." Many interns, when asked to express their concerns, wrote about issues such as getting enough people to attend a program, adequately connecting with people, and so on. Supervisors responded by confirming the appropriateness of such concerns, as if to say, "Yes, ministry is just really hard sometimes." Then they praised the intern by saying things like, "You did really well given the circumstances and despite the pressures you were under." Does praise sometimes get used to cover anxiety on the part of praise-givers for the hard things they are asking their students to do? Indeed, upon reflection, one supervisor pointed out that praise may be a way for him to mask the anxiety of "the intern inside him"!

Second, few supervisors contained themselves to simply telling what they saw. Many tended to heap on adjectives, for example, "When I watched, I saw a mature, graceful, and devout person." "Marianne is a wonderful communicator — poised, clear, funny, and not afraid." "Shelly shows a natural gift for preaching — she wants to be in this role." I found it very common for supervisors to comment on how "natural" their interns seem at ministry. This sort of praise gets offered even and especially when interns have explicitly stated their discomfort or trepidation. Clearly, these interns do not yet attribute their positive performance to their "nature," yet supervisors seem eager to make this attribution, rather than attribute the intern's success to hard work or strategies of improvement. When supervisors do note improvement, they tend to make blanket statements such as "She's come a long way in her preaching" without saying what that way was or how the student came along it.

---

5. I had 69 student-supervisor pairs that year, and each pair was required to do 4 reports throughout the year, so they produced 276 reports in all.

Some supervisors could not help but express their personal satisfaction with their intern. For example, one supervisor wrote, "Sean has been a joy for me to work with. We are a real team, easily sharing the tasks to be accomplished. Being able to rely on Sean has meant I could worship at the service myself." Occasionally, supervisors directed their comments toward me rather than the intern, saying such things as, "Thank you for matching Joe with me. This match has evolved into something much greater than I expected." To me, comments like these suggest that praise is often an expression of two other things — pride and gratitude — both of which reflect more on the praise-giver than the praised.

Finally, it is clear that clergy may simply have a hard time refraining from praise. Supervisors were given the option of letting a lay member of the intern committee or some other church leader do an occasional report. Without exception, these individuals gave more forthright and detailed assessments that avoided praise-laden language. For example, "The message was quite clear to me; however, Chris does tend to rush a bit." And, "I saw people genuinely interested in her presentation. The room was quiet with almost all eyes on the podium, which doesn't always happen [in this mental health setting]." Lay members may generally be freer of the need to express how proud and grateful they are for the intern's performance — perhaps because they have less riding on the intern's success — and can just get on with the business of feedback. I encouraged this year's group of interns to seek out feedback from people other than their supervisors (lay committees are not required in the Yale Divinity School program).

In contrast, the supervisors, who were usually clergy, tended toward generalized and flattering language. Instructed simply to offer feedback, some could not help themselves. For example, when asked for further comments, one supervisor wrote, "I don't want my comments about delivery to take away from the fact that overall Anne is a good, solid preacher." It is as though, like Carol Dweck's fifth-graders, they feel a need to rank their intern against all other interns, as if by not producing a favorable comparison they were responding inadequately. Almost without exception, supervisors used the space for further comments not to add further information but rather to make some praiseworthy summary comment like "Aaron has the potential to become an extraordinary preacher!"

I cannot help but wonder whether clergy, in contrast to lay people, are on the whole more committed to the idea that ministers are born, not made. They may be personally invested in the idea that ministerial qualities are fixed and given, to be discovered rather than cultivated, while the laity appreciate the hard work and dedication that goes into the making of a minister. Could it be that clergy cling to a "fixed mindset" about the gifts and callings to ministry because feeling gifted rewards them for labor that has few other rewards? Let us continue to reflect on this and other questions about ministerial formation and praise.

# - 11 -

# Constructive
# Congregational Feedback

*Teaching Ministry Students and Congregations
to Listen Well to One Another*

LOLETTA BARRETT, KAREN DALTON, KAREN CLARK RISTINE

Claremont School of Theology

**H**ONEST FEEDBACK from congregation members, delivered in a
context of mutual learning and care, can be a significant key to
growth in the practical skills and pastoral interactions of seminary
ministry interns. Creating the environment for such conversations
is both the hope and the challenge for the Teaching Placement
Committees in the field education program at Claremont School
of Theology.

Ministry interns are often subject to the same interactions with
congregation members and other staff in their field education settings as any pastor. Listening carefully during those exchanges, being
self-aware, being socially and contextually aware, while receiving
feedback and deciding whether and how to apply it in practice, are
critical skills for any minister.

The best Teaching Placement Committees in Claremont's program provide an opportunity for ministry interns to learn about the
practice of ministry through the experience of congregation members and to learn about themselves as ministers in relation to a
congregation. Skill-building goals in teaching, preaching, pastoral

caring, and other aspects of ministry are no longer isolated as an academic practicum; they become relational learning experiences. The challenge is to provide guidance that encourages and enables all settings to provide an atmosphere for these best-case conversations and interactions between congregations and ministry interns.

In our field education program, each placement site is required to provide a Teaching Placement Committee, whose purpose is to support and guide the student intern. The quality, commitment, and value of these committees, however, vary dramatically from site to site. When the committees work well, the experience and learning is enhanced for all involved. When the committees do not work well, the experience can be frustrating for the student, the site supervisor, and the congregation members, raising the question of whether the committees enhance or diminish the ministry intern experience. Early in 2007, Claremont's field education teaching team decided to give special attention to the Teaching Placement Committees to find ways to create field education experiences that are consistently constructive for interns and congregations.

## The Committee Structure and Process

While Claremont is a United Methodist seminary, students represent about forty denominations. Most field education placements are in congregational settings. Most Teaching Placement Committee members are lay people, and most of the supervising mentors are pastors of those congregational sites.

The Teaching Placement Committee is a group of four to seven people expected to meet monthly from September through April. The committee's work is intended to supplement and not duplicate that of the supervising mentor at the site. Claremont requires the Teaching Placement Committees to provide two evaluations of their interns during the year, describing the intern's work, the shared work of intern and committee, as well as observed strengths and areas for growth for the intern. The hope is that the committee will also function as a representative group, embodying the entire congregation's involvement with the intern while enhancing its self-understanding as a teaching congregation.

The supervising mentors are responsible for recruiting the committee from members of the congregation during the summer prior to the intern's arrival. The mentors are given suggested considerations for selecting members: diversity, commitment, involvement in the faith community, ability to keep confidentiality, good communication skills, and empathy. The mentors attend only the first committee meeting and guarantee that the committee and intern understand the expectations and process for their work. Together, the intern and chairperson are responsible for all subsequent meetings. The field education handbook offers suggested topics for the committee and intern for consideration.

## *Stories from the Field*

Teaching Placement Committees have the potential to provide field education interns with gentle, observant insight into their capacities for ministry, while also serving as friendly faces in the congregation, sometimes even serving as spiritual discernment guides. In the best cases, an intern's relationship with the committee will evolve and deepen over the course of the internship year as the intern is provided with candid reflection on both gifts and growing edges.

The committee's role is different from that of the supervising mentor, who makes assignments, sets expectations, and assesses outcomes. The committee's role also differs from the academic seminar instructor with whom the student meets each week on campus. The seminar instructor may elicit discernment questions but is primarily responsible for providing the setting for academic, clinical review and even dissection of key ministry moments and continuing concerns.

The Teaching Placement Committee stands alone in its ability to provide insight to interns from a congregational point of view and, in the best cases, includes members who help the interns feel that they have champions in the congregation, that they have someone in their corner.

That was the experience of Laura, a second-career seminary student in her fifties who relied on her field education in a Unitarian-Universalist Church as an intentional time of discernment. Her faith had conservative Christian roots; only recently had she found the spiritual center she was seeking within the UU community. She knew she felt drawn to leadership, but she did not know if she felt drawn to ministry. She shared this discernment issue candidly with her committee members and found them to be insightful guides throughout her discernment. By the end of her internship, Laura had decided to pursue candidacy for ordained ministry within the UU tradition.

Discernment is a key element in an intern's relationship with the committee. An attentive committee will ask the intern helpful questions and will help the intern form helpful questions for himself or herself. This is a different role from that of staff–parish relations committees or other lay-led committees with whom students will partner later in their careers.

Ideally, Teaching Placement Committees form before an intern arrives. Hopefully the mentor pastor carefully considers who in the congregation has insight into the congregation as well as gifts for teaching and mentoring. Sometimes a pastor invites a congregation member known for posing challenging questions and making astute observations. On rare occasions, where interns are assigned to churches where they already work, it is possible for the interns to participate in the selection of congregation members who are aware of their ministry.

Sometimes, however, the committee has not yet been formed when the intern begins to deal with real-life ministerial challenges. This was the case with Ellen, an intern in her late twenties who was assigned to a United Church of Christ congregation. Early in her internship, the partner of the church's pastor died unexpectedly. Ellen became part of the pastoral care support system and assisted the congregation through the pastor's bereavement leave. Her committee did not fully form until her second semester after they had already experienced her as an essential leader of their congregation. At the last service of her internship, the committee presented her with a robe and stole on behalf of the congregation, marking both their thanks and their recognition of her growth from intern to pastor.

The goals for each semester of a student's internship are set by the student in consultation with the supervising mentor and under the review of the seminar instructor at the seminary. The committee is aware of the goals, yet it does not set them and rarely monitors them. This allows the intern to talk more freely about the goals with the committee. Ideally, this also allows the committee to create an atmosphere for the intern to be able to critically and honestly reflect on any given ministerial setting.

Sometimes a committee will observe in wonder how interns successfully accomplish their stated goals. Kwan, for example, was already on staff at a multilingual United Methodist congregation in urban Southern California when he planned a key goal of his internship. He wanted his Korean congregation to host a 5K run. Some of his committee members admitted that they were not sure what such an event had to do with church. Kwan was determined to involve the church community in an event that would raise money for the concerns in the neighborhood: poverty, ministry to families of prisoners, services for senior citizens. He also wanted an event that focused on health, so the event included an eight-week training schedule that brought people together to prepare for the event. The committee members celebrated the success of the event and came to understand how such a race related to being church.

## Stories from the Field:
## The Committees' Experiences

Participation in the Teaching Placement Committee process gives congregation members an opportunity to take a mentoring role in the life of a future pastor. The capacity and desire to mentor another is one dimension of adult development and an experience that adds value to the life of the mentor, as well as benefits the one being mentored.

Claremont's field education director, Karen Dalton, had an experience that affirmed that experience. She was introduced to strangers by her friend, Ruth. "I'd like you to meet Karen," Ruth said. "She's a United Methodist pastor. I brought her up!" Ruth had been the chairperson of the staff–parish relations committee at the first church Dalton had served when she began her ministry career. Ruth, a member of that congregation for nearly sixty years, "brought up" many other pastors. In the past decade, she has also mentored four student interns from Claremont, serving as the chairperson for the Teaching Placement Committee. She takes joy and pride in the mentoring role she has played in these lives and the friendships that continue through the years.

Theological field education brings church people into partnership in the teaching processes, sharing the work of theological education with people outside seminaries. Wise lay people have an essential role in forming leaders for the church. The United Methodist denominational processes recognize this critical contribution as candidates for ministry are nurtured, named, and encouraged by their congregations. Seminaries receive students for only a few years and then send them into church leadership with the hope that they are prepared not only to serve and to lead but also to continue to learn from the people they serve and lead.

Teaching Placement Committee members benefit from the process in ways that sometimes are unexpected. Through conversations at their meetings with the intern, committee members increase their understanding of ministry and what seminary preparation for ministry involves. They develop a sense of partnership with the seminary, knowing they share in the vital formation of future leaders. They may also learn more about their own congregations and develop relationships with people they do not already know well.

One committee member offered this observation of the benefits she gained from serving on the Teaching Placement Committee:

Our intern presented what she was learning in seminary. She had people read chapters in some of her textbooks and she talked about her experiences at school. I never really knew before what people studied in seminary. I learned more about what the pastoral role is like, and it was nice to get to know her as a person. I had been in a class that she co-taught before, but I didn't know much about her as a person.

Another member of the same committee said:

I was impressed with the diverse and thoughtful people on the committee. It was not a group that would have come together otherwise, and I learned a lot about what different people think about the church and ministry.

Committee members are also often the ones best positioned to help interns understand what is expected in a given context and role. They can bring a combination of wisdom and caring when giving feedback about the need for change in an intern's work or behavior, or even appearance.

Students and interns both may have difficulty with the feedback and evaluation process. Committees that include only "cheerleaders" may not challenge the interns sufficiently, and, occasionally, there is a committee member who seems to be critical no matter what the intern does. New to the pastoral role, interns may be unaware of their strengths and reluctant to hear positive feedback, or they may resist and defend against suggestions for change.

## Stories from the Field: Problem Areas

The Teaching Placement Committee is expected to provide honest and constructive assessments of the intern's ministry and the interactions with the congregations. During this process and throughout the year, it is not uncommon for conflicts, concerns, and even prejudices to arise within the committee or congregation.

One illustration involves Leo, a Native American student intern who was assigned to a Native American congregation. Throughout his internship year, he spoke about the encouragement and support he felt from his supervising mentor pastor and the joy he felt serving a Native American congregation. Yet he also felt caught in an occasional undercurrent of prejudice. The senior pastor of the congregation was not Native American. Leo experienced this pastor as caring, competent, and committed to the church and its diverse congregation. However, Leo sometimes fielded comments — offered in the form of compliments — from congregation members who thought the church's senior pastor should be Native American. Leo believed that bringing these comments to his committee might add to division, so he shared them, instead, with his field education seminar on campus.

Confusion of roles and responsibilities, in addition to the temptation to triangulate rather than deal directly, can complicate the committee experience for interns and committee members. When problems arise, interns and committee members are sometimes unsure how to address them, and instead resort to avoidance. Neither the interns nor committees always understand the full role or the importance of this component of the field education program. While students reported getting feedback on their work in liturgy during Sunday services, some felt as if their committee members did not know about their work in the church beyond Sunday. One student suggested that committee members be encouraged or even assigned to attend classes, events, or community service efforts created or led by the intern.

A typical reaction of many congregation members asked to serve on such committees is that they do not feel that they have the needed expertise. They do not believe they know enough about theology or church leadership. They are unfamiliar with the seminary experience. The seminary does not always successfully convey how valuable their contribution is.

## *Toward Best Practices*

After reviewing the congregational committee component of our field education program, the Claremont teaching team decided to provide earlier, clearer, and additional information to the supervising mentors and committee members. In early July, each supervising mentor now receives a letter about the Teaching Placement Committee, its role and significance, and the importance of having the committee assembled and ready to go at the beginning of September. Guidelines about the committee's work and membership are included in the following letter from the seminary to the supervising mentor:

> The Teaching Placement Committee is a group of four to seven people whose purpose is to guide, support, and encourage the student intern. The committee is intended to supplement your work as a supervisor, in order to enrich the student's learning throughout the year. The presence of the committee can also help the congregation develop an identity as a teaching congregation, modeling so that others in the congregation come to understand and claim their roles in the education and formation of a future pastor. And the committee helps the intern understand and define the qualities of effective ministry as members of the congregation experience it.
>
> We ask that the committee meet monthly with the intern to give guidance, support, and feedback. The committee also participates in the evaluation process, writing a report and discussing it with the intern at the end of each semester.
>
> As you are recruiting committee members, we encourage you to seek people who:
>
> ◆ are faithful in worship attendance and participation in the church's ministry;
>
> ◆ have the time and interest to attend meetings and participate fully in the process;
>
> ◆ are diverse in age, race, gender, background, and involved in the life of the congregation in a variety of ways;
>
> ◆ will be well positioned to observe and experience the intern's ministry in the congregation;

* have empathy for others and good communication skills;
* will keep confidentiality and appropriate relational boundaries.

Effective Teaching Placement Committees will usually include cheerleaders as well as people who will sometimes challenge the student. A guideline is to include no more than one member of the staff–parish relations committee or other personnel committee. Members may be lay or ordained.

A letter addressed to committee members begins and ends with statements of appreciation for their participation. It also explains the Committee's role and emphasizes its importance. It concludes with an invitation to a field education orientation in August.

All the field education handbook materials, including the committee handbook, have been revised. We also have enhanced the Claremont website with field education in mind. Course syllabi, the field education handbook, and other related documents are now posted on the website and are available to all participants. The site also includes a section devoted to observations and suggestions.

The August orientation now includes more emphasis on the specific roles of the supervising mentor and the committee members, and each group receives these explanations simultaneously in order to be better able to give one another informed support and assistance. The program includes presentations by an experienced supervising mentor pastor and committee chairperson. A follow-up session in early November for committee members and supervising pastors provides more detailed training and resource materials after the groups have had enough experience with their intern to better engage the training. In addition to providing a letter and certificate of appreciation, Claremont also invites the supervising mentors and committee members to leadership conferences held on campus during the academic year.

In all of these ways, Claremont is working to raise the profile of the committees within the program, provide more complete information to guide them, offer ongoing training throughout the year, and express increased appreciation for the committees' contributions.

Claremont is also considering how to enhance the group leadership skills of both student interns and committee members. We plan to create an opportunity for the intern and the Committee to engage in a mutual ministry learning environment, an experience that will both strengthen the Teaching Placement Committee experience and prepare the intern and committee members for their future ministries.

## The Contribution of Teaching Placement Committees to Professional Personnel Committees

While the role of the Teaching Placement Committee differs from church committees with personnel functions, those two committees can be in conversation. Field education class meetings are intentionally structured on the model of professional clergy peer support groups, with the hope and intent that after seminary students will belong to a peer group that can support them and enhance their ministry. Similarly, the Teaching Placement Committee and the staff pastoral relations committee can learn from one another in ways that better prepare student interns for ministry and better equip congregational lay leadership for their assessment and support of their clergy.

To this end, Claremont will work with interns and Teaching Placement Committees to explore the resources that already exist for committees similar to the pastoral relations committees in their churches. The interns and committees will be encouraged to determine if a pastoral relations committee structure exists in their congregation and denomination. The field education program will then take the resources gathered from the various denominations and develop a model for Teaching Placement Committees with training for future interns, pastors, and committees. This training will include information about the denominational and congregational models of staff-parish personnel committees. An additional area of training and support will be for the mentors and the host churches as they select members for the committees and then provide formation and resources for them.

Using this approach will have several advantages. First, both the intern and lay persons will receive experience in committee processes and leadership while working on a shared project. Second, it will expose them to greater understanding of systems of support and communication that already exist in their denominations. Third, it will provide information on a specific method for increased communication between the congregation and pastor/staff, as well as increased support of the pastor, especially where pastoral relations committees do not exist. Finally, it will be a specific way for seminaries to assist the faith communities in forming and empowering leaders.

## *Conclusion*

Best practices regarding Teaching Placement Committees must include a number of dynamics. First, the committee, mentor, and intern must have a mutual and clear understanding of the role of the committee in the field education experience. Second, the importance of the committee meetings in the learning process for both the faith community and the intern should be understood and upheld by all participants. Third, the actual work of the committee must be clearly established at the beginning of the year and attended to throughout. Fourth, the program must provide specific training in group work or committee processes for committee members and interns, providing experience in working in and leading committees. When all of these are in practice, the field education experience will be more consistently positive for the interns and their faith communities, creating pastors and congregation members who listen well to one another and learn together.

# - 12 -

# The Use of Selected Texts for Theological Reflection for Ministry

MARY ANNE A. BELLINGER, MICHAEL I. N. DASH,
BETTY R. JONES,

Interdenominational Theological Center

I N THIS CHAPTER we will explore and reflect on the task of theological education, how field education contributes to that ongoing task, and specifically how through the use of selected texts — writings other than the biblical literature — we engage in theological reflection. We interpret our seminal and continuing task as a comprehensive formation of persons who can demonstrate the nexus between rigorous academic theological preparation and the practice of ministry in and through faith communities.

## *Interpreting the Task*

We understand our task in the Ministry and Context program at the Interdenominational Theological Center (ITC) as contributing to theological education. We set forth this task in a primary goal statement: the development of self-evaluative, critical theologians engaged in faithful and obedient ministry. This statement is presented to our students as they enter the program. We anticipate that our students, like us who are and seek to be engaged in ministry, will develop a mode of self-examination in all areas of their lives.

139

This means constantly reflecting and raising questions through self-evaluation and discovery about how students use words, use and care for their bodies, and most of all how they live lives in the totality of their being.

We expect our students to be critical theologians raising questions about the presence of God in their lives. They must constantly witness to ways in which they are being shaped and guided by relationship with and commitment to Jesus Christ. The journey in our preparation of persons leads to engagement in faithful and obedient ministry. As we seek to fulfill our task, we are assisted in our work by an examination of the recent and significant study on theological education by Charles Foster and his research colleagues.[1] In *Educating Clergy: Teaching Practices and Pastoral Imagination,* they note that the distinctive pedagogical outcomes of theological education are the interpretation of texts, the formation of pastoral and priestly identity, contextualization of information learned, and practices and performance of ministry. Foster and colleagues discover that the classroom allows educators to engage students in pedagogies of formation. "Many student respondents... expressed appreciation for teachers who foster in their classes dispositions and habits that explicitly integrate religious knowledge, clergy identity and character."[2]

## Theological Reflection
## and Its Contribution to Our Work

An important part of habit formation for priestly and pastoral identity includes ongoing theological reflection. Theological reflection enables one to test and confirm one's vocation to ministry. It offers occasions for the student to develop a sense of personal identity

---

    1. Charles R. Foster, Lisa E. Dahill, Lawrence A. Golemon, and Barbara Wang Tolentino, *Educating Clergy: Teaching Practices and Pastoral Imagination* (San Francisco: Jossey-Bass, 2006).
    2. Ibid., 101.

while fostering effectiveness for ministry. Indeed, theological reflection helps the student to address basic questions related to vocation, identity, tradition, experience, context, meaning, and action.

Theological reflection invites the minister to recognize and appreciate the human and theological dimensions of various life situations, which present pastoral opportunities, responses, and responsibilities. It is also through this process that contextual analysis is deepened, and the immensely important connection made between our theological ideas and our lived faith. Ongoing theological reflection fosters growth in ministry, both in terms of personal identity and practical effectiveness.

## The Objectives for the Course and Exercises

In order to fulfill our task as we engage in theological reflection on ministry, we identify the following as objectives in our syllabus:

Foster and enhance spiritual growth, theological development, and professional competence.

Explore different understandings of ministry and begin to articulate a theology of ministry.

Explore at several levels the interconnection between call, education, and ministry.

Develop skills in doing theology in ministry and encourage formation of a mode for doing theological work.

Provide opportunities for integration — theory and practice, concepts and skills, critical theological reflection and action.

These objectives address the major tasks of theological field education — interpretation, formation, performance, and contextualization — and contribute to the commensurate pedagogies in theological education as identified by Foster. We challenge our students to engage required texts with particular practices of textual interpretation that enable them to think critically and do theology in ministry. Students explore how the interpretation suggests choices for performing acts of ministry in their ministerial placements and other contexts.

Our learning objectives are realized over the course of two semesters. The focus of the first semester is on selected texts and readings for doing theological reflection. We continue this process in the second semester, where the focus shifts to class presentations of issues in ministry that arise from their placements. Students want to reflect upon what happens in their placements as they discuss the assigned reading, integrating assigned reading with practices of ministry. The learning experience of theological reflection on selected texts includes discussion of how the texts make a connection to what happens in the contexts in which they functioned. Students are challenged to illustrate how the selected texts, other resources, and theological reflection on activities in their placement enable them to be formed as critical theologians, engaging in faithful and obedient ministry.

Our design for the use of texts was informed by Dale Martin's essay "The Myth of Textual Agency" in which he argues that texts do not carry meaning in themselves. "My scholarship ...has attempted to highlight the activities of interpretation by which people *make meaning* of the biblical texts. I have insisted that the texts don't speak — except in the most tenuous of metaphorical senses of that term — and that we human beings have to do a lot of the hard work before they have any meaning for us at all."[3] Similarly, we believe that there is a dynamic of relationships that enables us to interpret and make meaning of any texts, biblical or otherwise. The reader comes to the text with a set of experiences that immediately begins to interact not only with the text, but also with the context.

We integrated Dale Martin's ideas with Carlos Mesters's basic model for Bible study in base communities in Latin America.[4]

---

3. Dale B. Martin, *Sex and the Single Savior: Gender and Sexuality in Biblical Interpretation* (Louisville: Westminster John Knox Press, 2006), 1.

4. Carlos Mesters, "The Use of the Bible in Christian Communities of the Common People," in *The Bible and Liberation: Political and Social Hermeneutics,* ed. Norman K. Gottwald (Maryknoll, N.Y.: Orbis Books, 1983), 122.

Mesters suggests that we come to the text with our life circumstances and situations. This is how we begin to appropriate meaning in the text. Mesters claims the biblical text is important, but no longer central to the meaning-making process for the lives of persons in the communities where he led Bible study, most often poor, rural campesino villages or urban *favelas*. He realized "that when the three elements are integrated — Bible, community, real-life situation — then the Word of God becomes reinforcement, a stimulus for courage and hope."[5] Wrestling with the biblical texts and other writings is useful for doing theological reflection on the contextual realities and as prelude to appropriate response in the practice of ministry. This reflection upon the texts is also a communal project.

Mesters's basic model, presented in this diagram, has been adapted for our purposes in doing theological reflection on ministry.

**CON-TEXT**
The community of faith
The community of the world
The arena of interaction of persons and engagement in ministry

Interpreting
Understanding
Acting/Doing/Working

**TEXT**
The shared vision of the life of faith
The sources of knowledge of the faith
(Scripture, tradition, doctrine, culture)

**PRE-TEXT**
The lived experiences
(of/for actors and persons)

In our adaptation of Mesters's model, we challenged our students to examine the material in the text selected for our class in the light of the pre-text, or everything they brought to the text: their experiences

5. Ibid., 123.

shaped by the numerous contexts, communities, and experiences of their lives. Interpretation and theological reflection for ministry occur within these interrelated relationships and situations between and among the pre-text, text, and context of ministry.

## Pedagogy for Using the Texts

Students grasp the concepts and affirm the usefulness of the model in helping them to engage the texts. We also provide questions as a way of guiding and shaping the discussion. Students grow comfortable with the process and begin to discover its value. They are encouraged to develop their own questions, to explore ways in which the texts enable them to form the habit of doing theological reflection. The following generic questions are proposed to guide the process and start discussion when the readings are considered in class:

> In the assigned reading, what set of ideas or concepts grabbed your attention and stayed with you?

> What forced you to examine your character as a follower of Jesus Christ, a person already ordained or seeking ordination, or one who understands ministry as vocation?

> What challenges do those ideas present for you and why? What changes are being suggested for redirection or new directions from your current way of life?

> What first steps in response are you willing to make? How will that commitment enrich your faithfulness and obedience to Jesus Christ?

> How does your reading of the texts suggest attitudes or postures you should assume as you seek to respond to ministry situations in context?

Indeed, we discovered that these questions led to other questions, offering students new ways of looking at themselves and of examining the appropriateness of their responses to the challenges and situations they encounter.

Our classes are divided into small groups of four to six persons, depending on the class enrollment. Students are invited into a covenant relationship in the learning community and for the work that they will do in groups, part of a formation process. These small reflection groups offer students a way of belonging to community, working with others, and being accountable to one another. Students in each group consult among themselves during an appointed class session or other opportunity. The task in the groups is to work together to prepare for leadership of class sessions. The leadership responsibilities include developing a brief devotional for a centering moment and providing reflections to start the conversation on the assigned readings. In the second semester, class presentations are focused on issues in ministry that specifically arise from one of the placements that the group has chosen.

Group members meet several times to determine how best to present reflections on the assigned texts. This is a focus in the first semester, although reflections on what is going on in their placements are encouraged. In the second semester, the emphasis is on a ministry issue from the placement site of one of the members from each group. A good presentation lasts nearly thirty minutes, and each group member participates in the presentation in a group-selected format. Full classroom participation in the discussion is encouraged after each presentation.

## Evaluation for Determining Outcomes

In the Ministry and Context program, students are provided with a copy of an instrument used for evaluation of the class presentations. The evaluation tools help clarify readings and issues from the ministry context, while examining how the readings also function to promote critical theological reflection on the students' ministry practices. Other sources of evaluation have included theological reflection journals. Students are encouraged to make entries in their journals that illustrate how they are reflecting theologically on their contexts and how those reflections make meaning for them regarding their pastoral identity and their growing understanding of their relationship with Jesus Christ. Additionally there are the usual papers.

## *Examples of Selected Texts*

Selected texts provide the foundation for group interaction in which students are challenged to engage the text. We are intentional in our program at the ITC to ensure that our choices of texts used in field education include women and African American scholars. The combination of textual exploration and group interaction opens a window for enterprising students to experience a renewed and deepened sense of servant-leadership. The texts we use include:

Howard Thurman's books of meditations, *Disciplines of the Spirit* and *The Centering Moment.*[6] Thurman has been considered the dean of African American theologians. A number of his works have made their way into syllabi of many courses in our ITC curriculum. Thurman's ideas, and the intriguing way in which he presents them, engender theological reflection and assist students in their formation and engagement in ministry.

*The Return of the Prodigal: A Story of Homecoming.*[7] In this book, Henri Nouwen provides a wealth of ideas for theological reflection from different angles. Readers are encouraged to see the fallen world through the eyes of God's redeeming love. Using the theme of homecoming, Nouwen explores the ways we respond to Jesus Christ, the ways Christ responds to us, and the ways we understand our commitment to his calling.

Renita J. Weems's *Listening for God: A Minister's Journey through Silence and Doubt.*[8] Weems uses narratives and reflection on her experiences to invite readers to wrestle with the question of what one does during the times of apparent spiritual disconnect

---

6. Howard Thurman, *Disciplines of the Spirit* (Richmond, Ind.: Friends United Press, 1987); and *The Centering Moment* (Richmond, Ind.: Friends United Press, 1990).

7. Henri J. M. Nouwen, *The Return of the Prodigal: A Story of Homecoming* (New York: Doubleday, 1992).

8. Renita J. Weems, *Listening for God: A Minister's Journey through Silence and Doubt* (New York: Simon and Schuster, 1999).

from God, the times in between when we last heard from God and when we will hear from God again. *God Don't Like Ugly: African American Women Handing on Spiritual Values.*⁹ Teresa L. Fry Brown recalls her family and upbringing in this volume. She writes about each person bearing his or her burden, acknowledging it, dealing with it. This process can lead to meaning-making and be a route to healing, wholeness, and restoration, as it enhances our capacity for building relationships with others. Fry Brown examines the spiritual values and moral wisdom handed on by grandmothers, mothers, and other mothers.

We also rely on Mary Monroe's book of the same title, *God Don't Like Ugly,*¹⁰ a story set on the streets and porches and in the parlors of Ohio in the 1960s and 1970s. It is the honest, hard story of Annette Goode, a shy, awkward, and overweight child who keeps a terrible secret. This story helps students realize how many young adults like Annette are members of their congregations, families, and communities. Reflection on this text helps us develop a list of twenty questions focused on ministry with wounded youth.

To address topics of call and vocation, we use *Ascent into Hell*¹¹ by Andrew Greeley and *Go Tell It on the Mountain*¹² by James Baldwin. Many theological issues are raised by the different subplots in both stories. Multiple dimensions and tensions in family relationships are examined. Both novels are also accounts of spiritual pilgrimage, of the discovery of God's grace and love during difficult journeys.

Novels can be employed as social commentary on the human condition and sources for reflection on religious experiences. African American writers regularly illustrate this nexus between religion and daily life. In their portrayal of African American life, they present the problems, tensions, excitements, struggles and joys. They show how

---

9. Teresa L. Fry Brown, *God Don't Like Ugly: African American Women Handing on Spiritual Values* (Nashville: Abingdon, 2000).

10. Mary Monroe, *God Don't Like Ugly* (New York: Kensington, 2000).

11. Andrew Greeley, *Ascent into Hell* (New York: Warner Books, 1983).

12. James Baldwin, *Go Tell It on the Mountain* (New York: Dell, 1952).

deeply embedded religious beliefs are both communal and individual resources for responding to life's challenges.

## Student Evaluations

To determine learning outcomes, we use evaluation instruments common to all courses in our curriculum. These results are collated and reported to faculty. We use these results to make modifications in the delivery of our courses and in our Ministry and Context program. In addition to these evaluation instruments, we provide opportunity for verbal feedback in the last class session of the semester. We ask students to share their perceptions of how the course objectives were realized, what were valued moments and occasions, what were missed expectations. Student responses reveal many of the values of this careful and communal attention to the use of texts in field theological education. Students readily observe how the group work broadens the scope of ideas, affirms their personhood, and strengthens their capacity to express themselves. The entire process increases their capacity to be intentionally self-reflective, to deepen their understanding as one called into ministry, and to understand their own vulnerability as a servant and leader. They also note how this process brought their learning from other classes into a new perspective and integrated their academic learning with their experiences of ministry. Students further observe that the readings and interpretation of those texts began to assist them with analysis and practices of ministry in their contexts. These comments express a significant discovery that students made as they engaged in theological reflection and the practice of ministry: the life of faith requires total investment of body, mind, and spirit.

## Conclusion

Discomfort sometimes makes it easier for us to theologize rather than critically reflect on who we are, who has called us, and what it means to be a pastor, teacher, and servant of the people. Through explorations of theological reflection using carefully selected texts,

ITC has formed communities of students, safe places where students can be heard and can exercise their true selves-in-formation. Each small reflecting group is a place to delve into their deeper thinking and challenges.

This process reinforces our commitment to the ongoing task in theological education: developing pedagogies of interpretation, contextualization, formation, and performance. Even though at different stages in our work we place varying emphasis on one or other or combinations of those pedagogies, each is equally important. However we choose to do theological reflection, our persistent concern is to demonstrate how the interpretation of texts deepens our understanding of the presence of God in our own lives, in the faith communities and other agencies through which we fulfill our calling. This expectation cannot be realized apart from careful analysis of the context in which ministry takes place, the needs of persons in that context, and recognition of the demands that our vocation places upon us for response. Yet perhaps more important than the sophisticated analysis of the context is the willingness of ministering persons to place themselves at risk on behalf of the insecurities of others. Further, our response — what we do, how we act and perform — will always be guided and shaped by our formation as servants of Jesus Christ and the ecclesial traditions and texts we embrace.

# – 13 –

# Reflective Theological Leaders

## W. J. BRYAN III, ISABEL N. DOCAMPO,
## BARRY E. HUGHES, THOMAS W. SPANN

### Perkins School of Theology

D ISCOURSE IS THE LENS that best describes the values and
method the Intern program of Perkins School of Theology
upholds as it reaches for the goal of equipping women and men to
become leaders with the skills and discipline to engage critically in
theological reflection as they partake in the practice of ministry. Discourse is a deliberate, deconstructive, and constructive engagement
that emerges from life's questions and aims to develop an aptitude
of searching for God, naming God's presence, and being known by
God, i.e., theological reflection.

The definition of "discourse" in this instance borrows from
anthropologist Clifford Geertz's discussion of "thick" ethnography.
"Thick description" means to engage in an ongoing exploration
of multiple and multilayered meanings, influences of context on
behavior, and ideas essential to analysis and interpretation. This
type of exploration leads to discourse *with* instead of discourse
"to" and "of."[1]

In the context of a theological field education program, students,
mentor pastors, congregations, and faculty are invited to engage

---

1. Clifford Geertz, *The Interpretation of Cultures* (New York: Basic Books,
1973), chapters 1 and 2.

in this ongoing, collaborative thick discourse. This is the theological reflection and pedagogical method woven throughout the Intern program and described in this chapter.

## *Overview of Pedagogy*

"Jane," a bilingual young woman with an excellent academic record, began her internship as an associate pastor intern at a medium-sized congregation. Jane clearly articulated her vocation to ordination as deacon in the United Methodist Church as opposed to elder. In the first month, Jane was thrown into a church conflict situation, to which, to her surprise, she responded with exceptional pastoral authority and leadership. This became the focus of her theological reflection with her pastor, the feedback sessions with her lay committee, and the conversations with her intern peers and faculty.

The faculty of the Perkins Intern program asks interns to understand their ministry practice as the subject of a mega[2] theological discourse encompassing both the intellect and the spirit. They are asked to lift out the details of their day-to-day ministry experiences that cut across gender, age, race, and class for theological discourse with multiple partners by writing theological reflection papers throughout the year. In these papers, students enter into "thick" discourse/reflection that initiates ongoing exploration of issues without a predetermined theological and/or experiential destination. This type of discourse helps interns come to terms with the inexactness, at times, of the role of the clergy; the complexity of theological-ethical issues at the heart of ministry; and a way of knowing theology (*habitus*) that seeks a fresh discovery of the nature of God.

This ongoing exploration through theological discourse with multiple partners is carefully integrated within the design of the internship. As already noted, the intern begins the discourse by submitting weekly theological reflection papers to the mentor pastors.

---

2. The term "mega" is used to refer to discourse and conversations that are very large in scope and depth.

This develops a habit of collaborative, reflective theological reflection in the midst of ministry. Second, the intern meets monthly with the Lay Teaching Committee for feedback that includes theological discussions of the meanings behind the practice of ministry and the student's growing identity as a pastoral leader. Third, the intern meets weekly with peers in a growth group led alternatively by the intern faculty and a psychologist for peer theological reflection and support. Fourth, the intern writes a Learning Covenant that guides the practice of ministry and the monthly Lay Teaching Committee feedback sessions. Fifth, the intern participates in a mid-point and final evaluation conference led by the intern faculty. Sixth, the intern faculty annually designs four Mentor Pastor Colloquies held on-campus for theological support and guidance to pastors as they supervise interns. Seventh, the intern faculty annually convenes with the psychologists who co-lead growth groups and consult privately with interns. These annual convocations stimulate theological discourse between psychosocial issues and clergy life. Eighth, the intern faculty meets regularly to share research and resources that have implications for the pedagogy.

The curriculum's *core* is the design and implementation of the intern's Learning Covenant. This design brings together each component described above so that what is being learned can lead to a broader vision. This mega theological discourse occurs at the faculty-led mid-point and final evaluation conferences. All parties — intern, laity, mentor pastor, and faculty — are convened to collect the wisdom from the ongoing multi-layered discourses that have taken place with multiple partners. An important outcome of the conferences is the opportunity to redesign the Learning Covenant in light of what this mega theological discourse illuminates as important areas for growth. Oftentimes, the practical and theological insights gained impact both the intern's post-graduate life and the church's ministry. The moment interns fully know themselves in relation to their Christian vocation and the larger church at work in the world is liberating — even when they choose not to pursue an ordained vocation.

Jane wrote in her mid-point evaluation, "My growth in pastoral formation has come in my understanding of the authority given to a pastor and in the importance of claiming that authority." At the mid-point evaluation, the lay committee was unanimous in reporting that Jane had already become a pastor with exceptional leadership abilities. The following six months, buoyed by the lay committee's feedback, Jane exercised leadership that guided the congregation to act on their potential instead of dwelling on their deficits. Subsequently, they excitedly began a ministry with Latino mothers and children. In her final evaluation paper Jane wrote that the ongoing reflection and discussions with the lay committee, pastor and peers about the various ministry tasks she performed enabled her to coalesce her understanding of the mission of the church and of her role in that mission. As a result, after the final evaluation conference, Jane sought ordination as an elder. The church, meanwhile, enthusiastically received a new pastor with a vision for community ministries.

The Learning Covenant, as seen in Jane's story, is key to the pedagogical lens of collaborative theological discourse. Without it, the mega theological discourse will be lost, leaving the particular discourses to remain isolated reflections, unable to render a more complete vision of what has transpired in the life of the intern and the church.

## Challenges

The pedagogical lens of collaborative discourse in theological education, as noted, guides students to integrate the classroom courses into the reflective practice of ministry. Nevertheless, the pedagogy has several challenges.

1. *Keeping the discourse open to voices who are not readily at "our" table — voices of the margins*

When a Perkins student becomes eligible for internship, that student more than likely is placed in a homogenous setting because the number of cross-cultural placements is very limited. In any given internship year, the majority of interns are white, United Methodist, and middle class. Consequently, the social context for education predetermines the shape of any discourse. This is not to suggest that non-white, non–United Methodist students do not make appreciative contributions to their setting and to the theological education; of course they do. These persons, however, are at risk of not being heard or valued in a larger forum of conversation due to the prefabricated majority cultural context. Such prefabrication raises the following questions: Whose table is it, really? Whose theology is at the head of the table? Can other theological views be at the head of the table? Why does there need to be a head in the first place? Is the round table a preferable image?

These questions challenge the single theological tradition that has largely shaped the Perkins Intern program. Theological considerations from the "margins" receive intellectual assent; however, that assent has not led to a fundamental shift in our theological orientation as chiefly expressed through our program structures.

A crucial consideration of theological discourse is revisiting who is at the table. Given our lip-service to diversity and our claim to being open to God's brand new future, perhaps it is time for a new table built by the hands of those who have historically been left out of shaping this program and the theological institution of which it is a part.

2. *Keeping the discourse open to how culture, classism, racism,*
   *and sexism form our perceptions of the nature of God and,*
   *subsequently, our practice of ministry*

There is a growing consensus in the academy that social location matters. Our social, economic, cultural, and educational backgrounds play a crucial role in providing the lenses through which we see the world and God. Our historical context informs our thinking. Truth becomes a socially historical experience rather than a universal abstraction that only a few privileged persons access.

The notion that race, culture, class, and gender are theological categories pivotal in subjective interpretation of doctrines is still debatable in theological education. Advocates of this notion are often generically labeled "liberationist" in order to draw suspicion to their motives and to the quality of their work. In spite of the politics surrounding the challenge, the Perkins intern faculty members believe social experience and personal identity are inseparable from the intellectual and practical work of ministry. This is a perspective that is at the heart of our work with students.

Students who are growing into this claim for their theological understanding find themselves out front of most members in their congregations. Some students, seeking to be true to their newfound convictions, may try to translate, if not transport, some of the implications of this theological methodology to their pastoral ministry and discover a variety of responses. In a theologically homogenous church culture, it is hard to introduce, let alone sustain, openness to a theological approach that not only asserts, for example, that race and culture shape our understanding of God, but changes the church's practice of ministry.

Students who take seriously race and culture in their theology of ministry may find that some laity engage in long-distance evaluations of the school based on what they hear and see in Perkins interns in the field. Nevertheless, discourse on how persons form perceptions of the nature of God across culture, race, and gender is consistent with the school's mission of preparing women and men for faithful leadership in Christian ministry.

   3. *Keeping the discourse open to God's revelation in the practice of ministry*

Theological reflection is both a communal and a personal endeavor. No one sees the whole in any given ministerial act. In truth, as finite creatures, we only see in part. Therefore, the thinking of others needs to complement our theological understanding. Conversation with others can give us new windows through which to value our ministry as well as grapple with our growing edges.

Without this critical conversation, there is the possibility of limiting God's revelation to one's own worldview to the exclusion of new truths. Healthy self-criticism can free persons from a posture of refusing to hear anything different from what they have previously been told.

Furthermore, this challenge is complicated when, for example, African Americans and/or Hispanics give voice to God's revelation, calling into question the norms and values of so-called established Western voices. African Americans, for example, by virtue of their historical experiences of trauma and rupture, have hammered out theological ideas that run counter to the theology that undergirds oppression and injustice. It would be a sin and a shame to argue that African Americans are ineligible candidates for the articulation of God's revelation in the world. And yet in subtle ways, this sin and shame may be more alive and active than most North American Christians want to admit.

The Perkins Intern program holds as a core value in theological reflection the notion that God values all persons. The program further asserts that there are various ways to perform theological reflection. No one method is crowned more worthy than another. The Intern program's present theological reflection model, well liked and well used as a method, must be open to critique. The intern faculty, while respecting the work of former intern faculty members in shaping the program's theological paradigm, must be open to the Spirit of God in forming new criteria and methodological elements for contemporary reflection upon the practice of ministry. The question facing the Perkins Intern program is: Can we honor and respect our deceased colleagues' memories and work by being open to hearing their hallowed voices saying to us, "Press on toward excellence; keep alive to the growing edge personally, professionally, and programmatically"?

4. *Keeping the discourse open to current research by our colleagues at Perkins in the fields of biblical scholarship, theology, history, and practical theology*

During the early 1990s, the late Dr. John Deschner talked about a "Third Perkins" as a way of applying a subjective grid to trends in Perkins history. The first Perkins existed through 1950. The second Perkins was the post-integration years. In both the first and second eras, Perkins boasted of having faculty members of wide-ranging stature in the academy and in the church. The language of a "Third Perkins" began to be used when the racial/ethnic and gender diversity of the faculty, as well as diversity in theological views, increased. Within the past few years, new faculty have joined Perkins in the areas of New Testament, Hebrew Bible, Pastoral Care, Christianity and Culture, History of Christianity, and Evangelism.

Annually for the last four years, the intern faculty members have hosted a luncheon for new faculty members. The purpose of this gathering is to introduce them to our program, share our philosophy of contextual education, and create partnerships in the common venture of theological education. From this informal gathering, the Perkins intern faculty has invited some of them to give lectures at Mentor Pastor Colloquies.

Other Perkins faculty members have been conversation partners in the conception and formulation of other pieces of the Intern program. These rich opportunities for dialogue have fallen short of intentional collaboration around contextual pedagogy. No regular forum exists, short of individual conversations in which the teaching faculty and the intern faculty collaborate on course designs or pedagogical methodology or research interests. Their research interests could impact future conversations on the shape of the Intern program, especially as they relate to common assignments or common areas of interest. Conversely, our expertise in leading theological reflection groups could impact the shape of course content, bibliography, and course methodology.

5. *Keeping the discourse open to freshness and creativity in our
conversations among the intern faculty*

It cannot be denied that freshness and creativity brought the
Perkins Intern program into existence. Throughout the program's
thirty-five-plus-year history, the intern faculty members have demonstrated spurts of creativity. For example, bringing the Concurrent
Internship option online demonstrated freshness and creativity. The
current intern faculty members also have engaged in less glamorous
perfecting and pruning of pieces of the overall internship models.

The challenge now is staying open to new possibilities in the face
of thirty-seven years of continuous success and affirmation in both
the academy and local churches. The gravitational pull of historical tradition is, in some regard, in tension with the Gospel pull of
freedom and creativity. Thus, the Intern program's future has to be
worked out in a vortex of passivity and possibility.

Change can be viewed as a gift or a threat. Choosing to view
this change as a welcome gift, the intern faculty engaged in discussions on how we do all aspects of our work. One of our colleagues
challenged us to have a zero-based approach to the program. What
would each of us envision if there was a blank page from which to
start? This is a question about trust. Three aspects of trust include
self, others, and the creative spirit of God.

Trusting self to be right is not as important as trusting self to
act in community. Behind the act is a person of gifts, strengths, and
broad experience. In truth, to act is a gift, but to be is a foundational
gift. Trusting the gift of self in a community of shared ideas is what
gives integrity to any group discussion. In a community of equals,
there should not be any concern about receiving ad hominems or
having one's offering devalued. The freedom to be oneself is as much
a harbinger of the future as are the achievements of the past.

Collegiality has been a hallmark of the Perkins intern faculty.
Each person's background and strengths are valued. This does not
mean relational struggles do not exist. Working together in such
a close and committed program makes for the real possibility of
differences in opinions. Differences in opinions and outlook are

constitutive of open dialogue among colleagues. The challenge the Perkins intern faculty faces in this regard is how to work out the deepest meaning of collegiality in such a way that all hands are holding aces and there is no trump card.

The language of freshness and creativity in a program that prepares persons for church leadership raises the issue of trust in the creative spirit of God. In a moment of lightheartedness, a colleague exclaimed: "I have an apostrophe!" The inside joke is that the colleague meant to say "epiphany." Epiphany happens. It is easier to trust an epiphany when the community is grounded in prayer, study, and theological consultation. A truism for us in supervised ministry is that a community that prays together stays together, and a team that consults together shares results together. In the midst of it all, God is at work — nudging, challenging, confirming, and always opening new paths into the future.

## Strengths

While the challenges are both pressing and formidable, the faculty of the Intern program at Perkins is full of hope regarding the future. We believe, even now, strengths within the program exist that will provide the space and energy for these challenges to be addressed in ways that give possibility to future paths.

The first challenge is truly a broad one. How does discourse function as "open" to voices not readily at our table? As wisdom proclaims: "It is what it is." In terms of race, we are in a predominately white context. The school of theology is 73.6 percent white, the university, 88 percent, the denomination that provides our major constituency of students, 92.2 percent, and its correspondingly clergy, 90 percent. In terms of gender, our program serves a denomination with a clergy population that is 79.1 percent male.

Yet along gender lines, for example, the student population at Perkins is more balanced than the denomination as a whole (48 percent female and 52 percent male). The present cadre of mental health consultants consists of white women and men as well as African American women. However, in the current corps of consultants, we have no African American male or Latino/a presence.

The intern faculty itself is composed of two white males, one African American male, and one Cuban American female. The larger faculty at Perkins School of Theology brings many voices to the table through professors who are white, African American, Latina/o, and Asian men and women. A 2007 report from the SMU Office of Institutional Access and Equity breaks down the tenured and tenure-track professors: sixteen male and eleven female; among the males, twelve are white, two are African American, and two are Latino; among the females, nine are white and two are African American. These professors teach from a variety of backgrounds and traditions, including United Methodist, Anglican, Presbyterian, Lutheran, Orthodox, Roman Catholic, and Baptist.

Special programs for academic credit include the Mexican American Program and the Hispanic Studies Program, as well as certificates in African American Church Studies, Anglican Studies, Urban Ministry, and Women's Studies. Through worship experiences within the community life of Perkins, students are exposed to a variety of styles and forms of worship across the course of each semester. In these ways, Perkins School of Theology gives students moving toward the internship experience various opportunities to encounter voices different from their own in a discourse we hope will influence both their understandings of God and the practice of ministry.

As is the case with higher education in general, and perhaps graduate theological education in particular, financial issues will continue to play a major role in helping to determine which voices are at the table and participating in theologically reflective discourse. Through an endowment, this program is able, to a limited degree, to subsidize internships across cultural, socioeconomic, and other traditional barriers.

Clearly this challenge will continue to loom before the program. There must be a constant and intentional commitment to bring as many voices as possible to the discourse. To that end, the SMU Strategic Plan for 2006–2010 includes the following objective

(Objective 3.1): "The Perkins internship faculty will investigate and implement ways to maximize the use of resources available in Dallas and elsewhere, including those of African-American and Hispanic churches, to help in providing contextual education and guidance in such areas as social justice, and report progress by May 2009."

The second challenge flows from the first. It is keeping the discourse open to how culture, class, racism, and sexism form our perceptions of God and, subsequently, our practice of ministry. Our program accepts that all theological understandings and, relatedly, all forms of the practice of ministry are culturally bound. To this end, not only in our campus classrooms, but also in the classroom of each intern's placement, students are challenged with developing vision that can see the social relationships and realities at work in even the seemingly mundane acts of ministry.

As previously stated, this aspect of theological reflection and discourse has been added to our work in recent years. The question, "How much is my image of God shaped by my culture, class, gender, and ethnicity?" is crucial for the development of sound and relevant theological thinking. Each of the papers an intern writes for the mentor pastor includes, by requirement, this crucial consideration. Through participation in the peer group classes, each intern will hear voices that do indeed speak from different places. In our current structure, the opportunity exists for the mental health consultant and faculty to press interns on the issues of how they relate to their ministry in terms of an awareness of culture, class, race, and gender.

Our program embraces the third challenge: to keep the discourse open to discovering God's revelation in the practice of ministry. This faculty believes the placement, or context, of internship is the primary textbook for the internship. The intern constantly faces the following questions: "What is God up to now?" "What is God doing in this place?" "What is God doing in my life?" "What is God doing in the lives of the individuals I am encountering?" And, in relation to the immediately previous challenge, "How do our social, economic, cultural, and educational backgrounds shape and color the God we see?" "Can we stretch beyond these factors to

catch a glimpse of the image of a bigger, more expansive God?"
The quest to discover and develop one's own ministerial identity is,
at its core, a journey of discovery. The program seeks to create many
different spaces within the life of the intern where these discoveries
can take place.

In the relationship with the Lay Teaching Committee, the intern
discovers new understandings of himself or herself and of God by
seeing life and ministry through the eyes of the laity. Through the
relationship with the mentor pastor, the intern experiences the surprise of discovery from one who walks where they long to walk.
In meeting and participating in the growth groups, interns discover
from each other new ways of being and doing. The time spent with
the mental health consultant, both in groups and individually, can
lead to powerful discoveries about the true self. Whether helping
the interns find their own identity as leaders, their own voices as
preachers and teachers, or their own hearts as champions for justice and peace, the Intern program is centered on discovering where
and how God works in specific contexts and in specific lives.

As previously stated, the internship is experienced through the
"Learning Covenant." At orientation, the faculty announces to the
new class of interns that this is the only class at Perkins for which
they write their own syllabus. The students are challenged to discover and combine: (1) what they most need to learn and that for
which they feel the most passion, (2) what there is to learn in the
context of their placement, and (3) what the course itself requires.
All these aspects are geared toward being open to discovering God's
revelation concerning the self, the church, and the world. With this,
the intern faculty is constantly sharing this journey of discovery as
well because there is no predetermined outcome of learning and
discovery. Each intern has his or her unique journey of discovery.
Through this practice, the faculty discover where God is speaking
in relation to shortcomings in present practice and also the need to
consider new directions for the future.

The fourth challenge is that of keeping the discourse open to
current research by colleagues in the fields of biblical scholarship,

theology, history, and practical theology. Theological field education struggles with how its place within the total academic curriculum of the theological school is understood. The full participation of the intern faculty in all aspects of academic life is important. In the program at Perkins, intern faculty serve on committees, participate in the search process for filling teaching positions, and function as full members of the faculty through division meetings. Through these personal and professional relationships such work and service develop, and collaboration is enhanced. Utilizing the expertise of the broader faculty in this work will lead, hopefully, to the larger faculty utilizing the expertise of the intern faculty in their work. As intern faculty, the time is now to claim our place at the table of discourse among the larger faculty through writing, research, and leadership.

The last challenge to be addressed is that of keeping the spirit of creativity and freshness alive in the discourse among the intern faculty. Working on a faculty team of four in the Intern program is a blessing. This creates relationships of discourse. The faculty share office space in a common suite, meet weekly for two hours, and share experiences both formally and informally throughout the course of each day. Each understands that part of our responsibility as faculty is to revise and improve the program, as well as the ways the work is done. Participation in the Association of Theological Field Educators and other professional conferences helps to sustain a sense of openness and excitement toward new ideas and methods of accomplishing evolving goals.

One way the discourse is energized at Perkins is through the shared leadership in the conception, design, and implementation of all major events across the calendar. These include a New Mentor Pastors Institute, Intern Orientation, two Lay Teaching Committee Orientation events, Consultants Convocation, and four Mentor Pastor Colloquies. This practice ensures no one person is the "keeper of all wisdom" and that each member of the faculty leads in a significant way in both the program as a whole and within the power structure of the faculty itself.

## Conclusion

This discussion raises several important questions the faculty needs to address. First, will the program commit the current financial resources to subsidize priority internships that bring the voices at the margins into the discussion, and will a commitment be made to secure more resources for future use in this manner?

Second, will the program make an ongoing commitment to have true diversity within the ranks of mentor pastors, teaching congregations, mental health consultants, and the faculty itself?

Third, will the intern faculty fully claim their authority within and among the larger faculty as "experts" in the specific field of theological field education and in the more encompassing field of practical theology? Will the faculty defer to those of other fields, even in those questions where both our ministerial and educational experience as a faculty and our work as theological field educators would give us authority to speak?

Last, in terms of the discourse among the intern faculty, the question will be whether we will dare to dream as boldly as those who have gone before and whose vision created the program as we know it today. Will the faculty be willing to let go of what is comfortable and known in order to grasp what might be disturbingly unknown in both structure and practice? Yet that is the heritage of the program. The strengths exist that can empower growth, change, and a deeper journey into the mission before us.

## Epilogue

Discourse shapes our community of theological field education. The table of discourse is round. The pulse of discourse is slow. The feasts of discovery and fasts of discipline encountered in discourse are always surprising. This allows the seminarian and all at the table to see faithful leadership in Christian ministry explored. Nevertheless, we must continually ask, are we ready and willing to be transformed by the offerings that each person brings to the table of discourse?

# Conclusion

## DAVID O. JENKINS

**A**s with similar projects, this book was limited in what it accomplished and what it could accomplish. For instance, the project reflects only the best practices of those schools invited to the 2007 conference, "Equipping the Saints: Best Practices in Contextual Theological Education." Readers likely observed that only mainline Protestant seminaries contributed. We lacked engagement from Roman Catholic, Orthodox, and evangelical seminaries. With only one historically black seminary attending the conference and writing for this volume, the project reflected this limitation as well. Even if most of the seminaries represented here have diverse faculty and student bodies, we do not know what practices African American seminaries would identify as unique contributions to the field of contextual theological education.

What difference does it make that all of these seminaries are Protestant? How do field education programs and supervised ministry experiences in Catholic seminaries differ from their Protestant counterparts, and how do we account for those differences? Does it matter that these seminaries are supplying future pastors for mainline Protestant denominations rather than evangelical free churches? If we had contributions from field educators in those seminaries, could we see if a significant difference exists in field education programs? Do Roman Catholic, evangelical, and African American theologies and congregational practices shape seminary contextual education in ways we can identify as particular to those traditions?

The book also is limited in that the accounts of best practices are first-person summaries and reflections. Each school has written about its own program without critical third-person perspectives.

Most of the participating seminaries could not identify a best practice particular to their school, let alone engage outside observers to help them see their program from other perspectives. A stranger living in our home for a week might observe patterns of behavior, dirt and dust we constantly overlook, cracks in the ceiling, as well as beauty, health, and vitality we take for granted. Each of our programs could benefit from outside observation, drawing on the collaboration and trust that the Association of Theological Field Educators has nurtured.

The need for third-party observation and review is linked with the broader need for program assessment. These chapters represent practices the seminaries *believe* are formative and successful, yet few of us have created the assessment tools that can measure that success. Seminaries sometimes survey current students or alumni, but the best we manage is anecdotal response, informative as that might be. It is difficult to quantitatively and qualitatively asses the skills we are developing in students through our field education programs, skills such as cultural competency, leadership, social analysis, the capacity to integrate practices of ministry with theological education, vocational discernment, as well as preaching, pastoral care, teaching, and administration.

We also have not invested the resources needed to study other disciplines — nursing, education, and public health, as three examples — to discover how those professions are evaluating the success of their field education. Our contextual theological education programs could benefit not only from researching evaluation tools from other professional schools, but also from inviting those professional educators and practitioners to observe and evaluate our seminary programs.

Another limitation of this project is lack of clarity and meaning around common vocabulary. Almost every seminary addresses "leadership," for example, yet we rarely state what we mean by leadership, how we came to define leadership in that particular way, how that definition implicitly and explicitly shapes our programs designed to educate and equip future leaders. More importantly, we also lack clarity about what we mean by "theology," "church," and "context." Although we presume a shared understanding, conversations with students, site supervisors, lay mentoring teams, and faculty reveal disparate meanings and applications, even after two or three years of participation in the same Contextual Education program. Even if we can never agree, conversations that expose our individual understanding are necessary for a variety of obvious reasons.

This project was also limited in that it did not adequately describe or evaluate the differences in the institutions that contributed to distinctions in the Contextual Education programs. For instance, we never addressed money, even though financial resources matter and influence every program. Staffing, student scholarships for international opportunities or internships, technology resources, and payment of supervisors and stipends for student field education placements are affected by the financial resources available to Contextual Education programs. Schools with large endowments for their field education or internship programs have opportunities other seminaries do not.

The size of the student body and faculty matters. Some seminaries are able to institute programs because they have a small number of students participating in their program, while other schools can create programs because of the hundreds of students engaged. Both are limited by size as well. Denominational requirements and expectations, varying curricular requirements, and university affiliation also have significant affect on what is valued, expected, and allowed.

Geography matters, too. Seminaries located in urban centers have different possibilities than seminaries in rural settings. The religious culture of the South has a particular formative influence different from the culture of the Northeast, Southwest, or Northwest. This project did not do any comparative analysis or ask authors to note how these factors shaped their programs and might have contributed to the best practices the schools developed.

Even with these limitations this project made serious contributions beyond the primary focus of displaying best practices in contextual theological education. It revealed that these seminaries are deeply committed to the formation of competent leaders for the church. Directors of Contextual Education programs are not passive administrators, but leaders thoughtfully engaged in the constant renewal of their programs. Because many of the current field educators have been in their positions for decades, they have developed practical wisdom regarding the formation of competent leaders for the church, even when research and data about their program success is lacking.

This project also revealed the vital partnership that exists between the academy and the church. Local congregations, pastors, lay mentoring teams, and judicatory leaders collaborate with seminary faculty and staff in the ministry of contextual education. This collaboration benefits both the academy and the church. Seminaries regularly host workshops for site supervisors and mentors that strengthen the congregational leaders' abilities not only to supervise seminarians, but also to function more effectively as the pastors and lay leaders of their congregations. These workshops and retreats also help create collegial communities among local leaders across denominational, racial, and class lines. Supervisors and site mentors often partner with faculty from across the curriculum to lead student reflection groups or contextualized courses, thereby engaging the supervisors in continuing theological education, while modeling for the students the rich conversation between congregational life and theological education. Congregations claim their place as mentoring communities, a task more complex and demanding than simply that of a laboratory for a seminarian's experience of ministry.

Seminary faculty and staff benefit from this partnership with the church by staying current with the movements and evolution of local congregations, as well as the change in demographics and realities of the broader social context. They also benefit from their reflection with congregations on how the seminary is actually educating and shaping seminarians for congregational leadership. The seminary critiques and complements the church. The church critiques and complements the seminary. When each institution values the other and enters into this shared work as a collaborating partner with shared goals, the benefits to the students are great.

Each of the programs represented in this volume shares an appreciation for the praxis-reflection model of contextual education, and a praxis-reflection model that is communal. Students are never asked to reflect alone on their experience of ministry, or to integrate their theological education with their practices of ministry without the accompaniment of peers, wise mentors and supervisors, and committed faculty. This practice is beneficial to students as a way of reflecting on their ministries throughout their careers. Field educators would likely agree that we hope students will be engaged in this way of doing theological reflection, of being a pastor and colleague, so that they will continue to be self-aware, self-critical, collaborating church leaders.

Finally, this project also reveals the deep commitments to social justice that exist in seminaries and particularly in the community of field educators. God's just commonwealth is *the* context for our work, shaping our values, goals, and hopes for our seminarians, as well as our hopes for the church and the world. As we help our students identify and address sin in the ways it inhabits individuals, systems, institutions, nation-states, and cultures, we are participating in the sanctification of the world. This book reminds us that contextual education does help equip the saints — seminarians, faculty, and congregants — to be God's faithful actors in the world. This book helps display these activities that are more than summaries of our best practices in contextual theological education. Because it does so, it is a gift of hope for the church.

# Bibliography

Albom, Mitch. *Tuesdays with Morrie: An Old Man, a Young Man, and Life's Greatest Lesson.* New York: Broadway Books, 2002.

Anderson, Gerald H., ed. "Karl Hartenstein 1894–1952: Missions with a Focus on 'The End.'" *Mission Legacies: Biographical Studies of Leaders of the Modern Missionary Movement.* Maryknoll, N.Y.: Orbis Books, 1998.

Baldwin, James. *Go Tell It on the Mountain.* New York: Dell, 1952.

Batts, Valerie. *Modern Racism: New Melody for the Same Old Tunes,* EDS Occasional Papers, no. 2 (Cambridge, Mass.: Episcopal Divinity School, 1998).

Becker, Therese M. "Individualism and the Invisibility of Monoculturalism/Whiteness: Limits to Effective Clinical Pastoral Education Supervision." *Journal of Supervision and Training in Ministry* 22 (October 2002).

Bellah, Robert Neelly. *The Good Society.* New York: Vintage Books, 1992.

Bellah, Robert N., Richard Madsen, William Sullivan, and Ann Swidler. *Habits of the Heart: Individualism and Commitment in American Life.* Berkeley: University of California Press, 1985.

*Book of Order: The Constitution of the Presbyterian Church (USA).* Part II 2007/2009. New York: Office of the General Assembly, Presbyterian Church (USA).

Bosch, David J. *Transforming Mission: Paradigm Shifts in Theology of Mission.* Maryknoll, N.Y.: Orbis Books, 1993.

Bronson, Po. "How Not to Talk to Your Kids." *New York Magazine,* February 19, 2007.

Calvin, John. *Calvin: Institutes of the Christian Religion.* Ed. John T. McNeill. Trans. Ford Lewis Battles (Louisville: Westminster/John Knox Press, 1973.

Carroll, Jackson W., Carl S. Dudley, and William McKinney, eds. *Handbook for Congregational Studies.* Nashville: Abingdon, 1986.

Click, Emily. "Forming Religious Leaders through Theological Field Education." Ph.D. dissertation. Claremont School of Theology.

de Mello, Anthony. *Awareness: The Perils and Opportunities of Reality.* New York: Doubleday, 1992.

DeMott, Benjamin. *The Trouble with Friendship: Why Americans Can't Think Straight about Race.* New York: Grove/Atlantic, 1996.

Dweck, Carol S. *Mindset: The New Psychology of Success.* New York: Random House, 2006.

Dweck, Carol S., and Claudia S. Mueller. "Praise for Intelligence Can Undermine Children's Motivation and Performance." *Journal of Personality and Social Psychology* 75, no. 1 (1998).

Farley, Edward. *Theologia: The Fragmentation and Unity of Theological Education.* Philadelphia: Fortress Press, 1983.

Fluner, Yvette A. *Where the Edge Gathers: Building a Community of Radical Inclusion.* Cleveland: Pilgrim Press, 2005.

Foster, Charles R., Lisa Dahill, Larry Golemon, and Barbara Wang Tolentino. *Educating Clergy: Teaching Practices and Pastoral Imagination.* San Francisco: Jossey-Bass, 2006.

Freire, Paulo. *Pedagogy of the Oppressed.* New York: Continuum, 1968.

Friedman, Edwin H. *Generation to Generation: Family Process in Church and Synagogue.* New York: Guilford Press, 1985.

Fry Brown, Teresa. *God Don't Like Ugly: African American Women Handing on Spiritual Values.* Nashville: Abingdon, 2000.

Geertz, Clifford. *The Interpretation of Cultures.* New York: Basic Books, 1973.

Gottwald, Norman K., ed. *The Bible and Liberation: Political and Social Hermeneutics.* Maryknoll, N.Y.: Orbis Books, 1983.

Greeley, Andrew. *Ascent into Hell.* New York: Warner Books, 1983.

Heifetz, Ronald. *Leadership without Easy Answers.* Cambridge, Mass.: Belknap Press of Harvard University Press, 1994.

Holland, Joe, and Peter Henriot, S.J. *Social Analysis: Linking Faith and Justice.* Maryknoll, N.Y.: Orbis Books, 1983.

Hopewell, James F. *Congregation: Stories and Structures.* New York: Fortress Press, 1987.

Hulstrand, Janet. "Education Abroad and on the Fast Track." *International Educator* (May–June 2006).

Irvin, Dale T. "Open-Ended Pedagogy in a Multicultural Classroom: The Case for Theological Education." *Religious Studies News* 4, no. 1 (February 1996).

Klimoski, Victor J., Kevin O'Neill, and Katrina Schuth, eds. *Educating Leaders for Ministry: Issues and Responses*. Collegeville, Minn.: Liturgical Press, 2005.

Kushner, Harold S. *Living a Life That Matters: Resolving the Conflict between Conscience and Success*. New York: Alfred A. Knopf, 2001.

Kushner, Lawrence. *Jewish Spirituality: A Brief Introduction for Christians*. Woodstock, Vt.: Jewish Lights Publishing, 2001.

Lossky, Nickolas, ed. *Dictionary of the Ecumenical Movement*. Geneva: WCC Publications, 2002.

Maduro, Otto. *Religion and Social Conflicts*. Maryknoll, N.Y.: Orbis Books, 1982.

Mann, Alice, and Gil Rendle. *Holy Conversations*. Herndon, Va: Alban Institute, 2003.

Martin, Dale. *Sex and the Single Savior: Gender and Sexuality in Biblical Interpretation*. Louisville: Westminster John Knox Press, 2006.

Monroe, Mary. *God Don't Like Ugly*. New York: Kensington, 2000.

Nouwen, Henri J. M. *Can You Drink the Cup?* South Bend, Ind.: Ave Maria Press, 1996.

———. *The Return of the Prodigal: A Story of Homecoming*. New York: Doubleday, 1992.

Palmer, Parker. *Let Your Life Speak: Listening for the Voice of Vocation*. San Francisco: Jossey-Bass, 1999.

Parks, Sharon Daloz. "Is It Too Late? Young Adults and the Formation of Professional Ethics." In *Can Ethics Be Taught? Perspectives, Challenges, and Approaches at Harvard Business School*. Ed. Mary C. Gentile, Sharon Daloz Parks, Thomas R. Piper. Cambridge: Harvard Business School, 1993.

Radillo, Rebeca. "A Model of Formation in the Multi-cultural Urban Context for the Pastoral Care Specialist," Sect. II. In *The Formation of Pastoral Counselors: Challenges and Opportunities*. Ed. Duane R. Bidwell and Joretta L. Marshall. Binghamton, N.Y.: Haworth Press, 2007.

Rich, Adrienne. *The Dream of a Common Language: Poems 1974–1977*. New York: W. W. Norton, 1993.

Ruiz, Lester Edwin. "Radical Inclusion: The Purpose of Cartography as Grand Theorizing." Essay presented at the International Christian University, Tokyo, June 1, 2007.

Schön, Donald A. *Educating the Reflecting Practitioner: Toward a New Design for Teaching and Learning in the Professions.* San Francisco: Jossey-Bass, 1987.

Smith, Archie. *The Relational Self: Ethics and Therapy from a Black Church Perspective.* Nashville: Abingdon, 1982.

Steinke, Peter L. *Healthy Congregations: A Systems Approach.* Bethesda, Md.: Alban Institute, 2006.

Taylor, Barbara Brown. *A Preaching Life.* Lanham, Md.: Cowley Publications, 1993.

Thurman, Howard. *The Centering Moment.* Richmond, Ind.: Friends United Press, 1990.

———. *Disciplines of the Spirit.* Richmond, Ind.: Friends United Press, 1987.

Weems, Renita J. *Listening for God: A Minister's Journey through Silence and Doubt.* New York: Simon and Schuster, 1999.

Wellman, David. *Portraits of White Racism.* 2nd ed. New York: Cambridge University Press, 1993.

Willimon, William. *Calling and Character: Virtues of the Ordained Life.* Nashville: Abingdon Press, 2002.

# Contributors

**Loletta Barrett** is a Teaching Assistant in Field Education at Claremont School of Theology.

**Mary Anne Bellinger** is a Facilitator for the Ministry and Context Program at Interdenominational Theological Center.

**Barbara Blodgett,** Director of Supervised Ministries, Yale Divinity, is the author of *Constructing the Erotic: Sexual Ethics and Adolescent Girls.*

**W. J. Bryan III** is Director of the Intern Program and Professional Formation and Professor of Supervised Ministry at Perkins School of Theology.

**Phil Campbell** is Director of Ministry Studies and Visiting Assistant Professor of Leadership and Congregational Studies at Iliff School of Theology.

**Emily Click** is the Assistant Dean, Ministry Studies and Field Education, and Lecturer on Ministry at Harvard Divinity School.

**Landis Coffman** serves as Pastor of Holy Trinity Lutheran Church in Akron, Ohio.

**Karen Dalton** is Director of Field Education and Dean of Extension Programs and Ministry Resources at Claremont School of Theology.

**Michael I. N. Dash** is Professor, Ministry and Context, at Interdenominational Theological Center.

**Mark Diemer** serves as Pastor of Grace of God Lutheran Church in Columbus, Ohio.

**Isabel N. Docampo** is Associate Professor of Supervised Ministry at Perkins School of Theology.

**Ruth Fortis** is Pastor to the Community and Director of Mentoring Ministries at Trinity Lutheran Seminary.

**Barry E. Hughes** is Associate Professor of Supervised Ministry at Perkins School of Theology.

**Martha R. Jacobs** serves as Adjunct Faculty at New York Theological Seminary.

**David O. Jenkins,** Assistant Professor in the Practice of Church and Community Ministries, Director of International Initiatives, and Director of Contextual Education I at Candler School of Theology, is the author of *Hospitality: Risking Welcome.*

**Jane Jenkins** is Associate Professor of Pastoral Theology and Director of Contextual Education and Internships at Trinity Lutheran Seminary.

**Betty Jones** serves as a Facilitator for the Ministry and Context Program at Interdenominational Theological Center.

**Viki Matson** is Assistant Professor of the Practice of Ministry and Director of Field Education at Vanderbilt Divinity School.

**Eleanor Moody-Shepherd** is Interim Director of the Doctor of Ministry Program, Associate Dean and Director of the Certificate Program, and Professor of Ministry at New York Theological Seminary.

**Rebeca M. Radillo** is Associate Professor of Pastoral Care and Community Ministries and Director of Supervised Ministry at New York Theological Seminary. She is the author of "The Embodiment of Enmity," in *The Living Pulpit* (2004).

**Lynn Rhodes** is Associate Professor of Ministry and Field Education at Pacific School of Religion.

**Karen Clark Ristine** is a Master of Divinity Student at Claremont School of Theology.

**P. Alice Rogers** is Assistant Professor in the Practice of Congregational Leadership, Director of Teaching Parish Program, and Director of Contextual Education II at Candler School of Theology. She is co-editor of *Contextualizing Theological Education* (Pilgrim Press, 2008).

**Thomas W. Spann** is Professor of Supervised Ministry at Perkins School of Theology.

**Joseph S. Tortorici** is Associate Professor of the Practice in Ministry and Mission, Associate Director of Practice in Ministry and Mission and Coordinator of Student Pastor Program at Wesley Theological Seminary.

**H. Stanley Wood,** Ford Chair Associate Professor of Congregational Leadership and Evangelism, Director of Field Education and Integrative Studies, San Francisco Theological Seminary, is editor of *Extraordinary Leaders in Extraordinary Times,* 2 vols. (Eerdmans, 2006).